BUYING OR SELLING A BOAT

BUYING OR SELLING A BOAT

Colin Jarman

ADLARD COLES LIMITED
8 Grafton Street, London W1

Adlard Coles Ltd
William Collins Sons & Co. Ltd
8 Grafton Street, London W1X 3LA

First published in Great Britain by
Adlard Coles Ltd 1985

Distributed in the United States of America
by Sheridan House, Inc.

Copyright © Colin Jarman 1985

British Library Cataloguing in Publication Data
Jarman, Colin
Buying or selling a boat.
1. Boats and boating—Purchasing
I. Title
623.8'2   VM351

ISBN 0-229-11719-8

Typeset by V & M Graphics Ltd, Aylesbury, Bucks
Printed and bound in Great Britain by
R. J. Acford, Chichester, Sussex

Contents

Contents

Contents

Preface

Buying a boat is no easier than buying a house or a car. There is an enormous variety of shapes, sizes and types on the market and sifting through them to find the one that best suits you and your requirements can involve hours of searching. It must be done though and it must be done carefully with as much information to hand as possible since boats are not cheap and they are likely to represent either a very substantial capital investment or a pretty big loan.

The aim of the first part of this book is to try to point the reader in the right direction, to guide their thoughts towards the goal of the right boat at the right price that will give them the satisfaction and enjoyment that only boating can. There are many considerations and many pitfalls, so the chapters are, of necessity, fairly broad in their coverage, but I believe it will help to smooth the process out.

In the second part of the book we look at the flip side of the business and turn to the selling of boats. Whether this is undertaken in order to buy your next boat or to give up boating altogether, the same matters must be gone over and the same processes undertaken, so again it is my aim here to clear the way and help you in the end to obtain a straightforward sale at the right price.

Even for those of us who have owned several boats and think we know something about the buying and selling of them, each purchase and each sale usually ends up as an emotional deal. We try to stand back and be dispassionate about the whole thing, weighing up the pros and cons and doing calculations about costs and insurance, but in the end we usually let our hearts rule our heads and either buy the boat that we fall in love with or sell her to the person we think will give her the best home – regardless of the price. That being the case it is even more important that we begin each purchase or sale with as clear a head as possible and it is the intention of this book to guide you towards a situation where, with closed ears and eyes, but open cheque book you will actually have made the right choice, or with open hand have found the right buyer.

I wish you luck and fun, because apart from the sport of boating, actually buying and selling boats can be fun.

Colin Jarman

Part 1
Buying A Boat

1. Choosing the Right Kind of Boat

The decision to become a boat owner and a decision on what kind or type of boat to buy are so closely linked that they form a 'chicken and egg' relationship. Some people daydream about the kind of boat they would like to own if they ever bought a boat and from that comes the firm decision to buy one, while others decide to buy a boat and then look at what they will actually get. It matters little which comes first, provided that in the end the right boat is bought.

What the right boat is depends on many factors: the kind of boating you are interested in; the expected level of involvement of any family and/or friends; the type of watersports available within a reasonable distance of your home; costs and personal finances; and so on.

What sort of boating?

Everyone's decisions have to be made, eventually, on the basis of personal tastes and circumstances, but in broad terms the kind of boating you want to become involved with – or perhaps are involved with, but now want to own a suitable craft to extend that involvement – must be the first thing analysed. Each area of boating has its own qualities, some of them appealing across boundaries (for example, many people with sailing cruisers also own a sailboard), while others stick rigidly to boundaries (for example, not many people combine sailing with circuit powerboat racing).

Each part of the general sport of boating has its own pleasures to offer those interested. The thrill of driving a small sportsboat at upwards of 40 knots can only be likened to driving an open-topped car on an empty motorway. In smooth water it is sheer exhilaration; in choppy water it can be a spine-jarring purgatory. Waterskiing offers a similar thrill to snow skiing (and many yachtsmen ski in the winter) with great skill needed to undertake single ski work, slalom and tricks. Dinghy sailing is often talked of as being *the* way to learn to sail and admittedly it does sharpen your reflexes – otherwise you go swimming as the dinghy capsizes – but for many adults, particularly those admitting to middle age, it is often better to learn in something with a keel that will forgive the odd mistake. You can always take to a dinghy after you have learned the rudiments of sailing.

Cruising with your family, whether in a motor cruiser or a sailing one, can either bring you all very close together, united by shared experiences and enjoyment of being afloat together, visiting new places and familiar haunts, or it can become an indulgence for the parents that is hated by the children, resulting in a deep family division. There is no guaranteed way to make a success of family cruising, but it must largely come down to an ability and desire on everyone's part to think about other members of the family and ensure that they too enjoy themselves. It is not unusual for father and son to want to go charging off to foreign parts despite a forecast of strong headwinds, while mother and younger children want to visit the local museum or spend the day on the beach. The decision about which to do must be tempered by the fact that it is supposed to be a family pleasure and the certainty that, once badly scared, people are going to be reluctant to go afloat again.

There is immense pleasure to be gained from making a passage to a new port, exploring it thoroughly and sailing on. It can also be refreshing and relaxing to lie at anchor in a quiet backwater watching the tide ebb and flow, counting stars and reading bedtime stories. Each may please only some of the family, but they can all profitably be experienced by the whole of a willing family.

The time will come too when a young family grow up and want to go out on a Saturday night with their friends. Then they and their parents will have to come to some agreement about how often the boat will be neglected in favour of the disco. And good luck to everyone in that debate!

For many boat owners the pleasure of ownership lies not so much in going to sea or even wandering far from the home berth or mooring, but in working on the boat, keeping her smart and maintaining the engines for the time when they *might* be wanted. People have been known to spend years building a boat only to sell her after one season afloat and start all over again building another one. Their boating fun is based on dry land and camaraderie in the boatyard, but they still feel a pleasurable part of the whole boating scene.

The recent explosion of boardsailing all over the world has opened up the pleasures of wind powered movement afloat (they are not exactly boats, so it's not exactly boating) to a host of people who would never otherwise go afloat at all. It makes use too of areas of water such as gravel pits and lakes that would probably not be used for anything else. It is a highly mobile sport as the boards are light and easily portable on car roof racks; they can be sailed as well by men as women, children as adults; in light winds and strong (depending on experience and common sense). It is a new sport that has largely been adopted by young people who have extended the surfing cult with all its colourful razzamatazz. Boards are often brightly painted; sails multicoloured and beach parties develop spontaneously.

Safety

The question of boating safety often arises, particularly when there has been some spectacular rescue by helicopter or lifeboat which has either been on TV news programmes or has had front page mention in the newspapers. At such times there are often calls for restrictions and tighter controls, cries which ignore thousands of people's perfect safety record each season.

Much emphasis is put on safety at sea by instructional handbooks and magazines, and rightly so, but it can be overdone. At a symposium on 'going foreign' not so long ago almost all questions from the floor were on tactics for coping with gales and heavy weather. Only at the end was one woman brave enough to ask the panel if they couldn't tell her just what fun a foreign cruise could be and how smooth the sea is occasionally. She was right. Seagoing is fun for probably 80% of the time, but it is the remaining 20% that frightens or at least preoccupies so many people and occasionally hits the headlines. The possibility of danger from whatever cause cannot be overlooked, but it must be kept in perspective. It's like breaking down on a car journey. If you worry about it too much you will never leave home.

What constitutes dangerous conditions varies from one type of boat to another and from the soundness of construction of one boat to another, apart from the strength or expertise of the crew. A rowing dinghy would be a most unsuitable craft to take out in open waters in a strong wind on a day's angling trip, but in the same wind a 30 ft sailing cruiser may be at her best. On the other hand, if two boats, one professionally built of top-quality materials and the other amateur-constructed of sub-standard materials, were faced with the same testing conditions, it is likely that the poorly built one would be in trouble long before the sound boat, even if their crews were of equal ability. And of course, a novice boardsailor trying to learn in an offshore wind may end up exhausted and in very serious trouble when a more experienced person is having a fine time.

Generally, however, it should be emphasized that boating is *enjoyable*. It does have to be taken seriously, but it is enjoyable. One of the most dangerous phrases anyone has come up with is the oft-quoted 'messing about in boats'. Don't mess about.

The right boat for the job

Now let's try to look at the purpose requirements of various sections of the general sport of boating.

Ski boats and runabouts

When you decide to buy a sportsboat for use either as a towboat for waterskiing or simply as a fast runabout you will be looking at broadly similar craft with large, powerful engines and planing hulls. The hull may either be shaped like a V (often called a Deep Vee hull) or in some sort of triple vee configuration (cathedral or triform hull). The Deep Vee type will have a softer ride in rough water as the vee shape cuts into waves as the hull drops down onto them, whereas the triple hull form will smack down sharply onto the water. However, particularly at rest, the triple hull is more stable than a Deep Vee one, staying more nearly level as people move about in the boat or as she is driven through corners. In both cases the hull flattens out to some extent towards the stern to provide a

Plate 1.1. *Sportsboat racing over circuits laid out on disused gravel pits, lakes and in dock areas is a popular motor boating sport requiring relatively low investment for a high level of thrills.*

planing surface; an area on which the boat rides at speed with the rest of the hull out of the water.

The powerful engines for these boats may be either inboards, outboards or outdrives. An inboard engine drives the propeller by way of a long, straight shaft running out through the bottom of the boat, while an outboard sits up on the transom entirely outside the boat and an inboard/outboard or outdrive splits the difference, having the engine inboard and a drive leg, looking much like the lower drive unit of an outboard, poking out through the transom. Broadly speaking, an inboard is heavy but reliable although its propeller is unprotected when the boat is beached; an outboard is lighter and can be tilted up out of the water to protect the propeller, but may not be quite as reliable as an inboard; and finally an inboard/outboard has the advantages of an inboard (but shares the disadvantage of taking up space in the boat) and overcomes the problem of propeller protection by having the tilting drive leg. Most smaller runabouts and ski boats have outboard engines, either a single one or a pair, but certainly an outdrive is worth considering for larger, possibly heavier craft.

For towing a waterskier it is far better to have a towing

Plate 1.2. *Many of today's top sailors started out in the International Cadet class, which is sailed by children up to the age of 16. These pram bowed dinghies are tough (they frequently take a lot of bashing as they round marks in tight bunches) and give their crews a lot of fun in addition, of course, to teaching them good basic sailing and racing skills. Between races at open meetings, both afloat and ashore, there is always a great spirit of camaraderie between the crews and between their accompanying parents.*

pillar, from which the tow line will stay clear above the outboard from whatever angle the skier is pulled, than a pair of eyes bolted onto the transom, one each side of the engine. This latter arrangement, often seen on runabouts sold with a dual role as skiboats, can also make driving difficult as the skier sweeps from one side to the other across the wake, since the sideways pull on the transom has a greater effect than the same lateral pull on a pillar in the cockpit.

The hull of any fast planing boat must be strong enough to withstand slamming in rough water and a certain amount of bouncing about on a road trailer, since virtually all such craft are towed to and from the water by road. This feature also requires a properly designed, built and fitted trailer of course.

Sailing dinghies

These can be divided into keelboats, class racing dinghies and dayboats. Your choice initially must depend on your sailing intentions, primarily whether you intend to race or not. If you intend to race there will be little sense in buying a class of dinghy that is not raced at the club you want to sail from. Obviously someone has to take the plunge if a new class is to be established, but for the most part it is better to see what boats are raced there and choose one of these.

Keelboats may require a mooring on which they lie afloat for the season as it is much harder to haul out a boat with a deep keel between races than it is one with a centreboard. Some clubs do 'dry sail' their keelboats, but they need good craning facilities. The majority prefer to keep their Flying Fifteens, Solings or whatever on fleet moorings near the clubhouse.

A centreboard dinghy will need a good launching trolley and possibly a road trailer as well for taking the dinghy to open meetings at other clubs or home for winter storage. The launching trolley need only have solid wheels without any axle bearings as it will be in and out of the water each time you go sailing and if that water is salt anything more sophisticated could soon deteriorate and seize up.

One very important decision regarding dinghy types is whether you intend sailing singlehanded or with a crew. Almost all singlehanders are centreboard boats but there their similarities end. Some have two sails (mainsail and jib), some have one; some have standing rigging to hold the mast up, some

Plate 1.3. *The Laser, one of the world's most popular and exciting singlehanded dinghies. They are raced widely and very competitively, demanding a high degree of skill and fitness from the race winner, but can also provide simple good fun for those not wanting to race. Easily carried on the roof of most cars, the Laser can be taken on holiday without problems and, perhaps because they are singlehanders, the owners are a very friendly and gregarious lot off the water.*

do not; some, like the very popular 10 ft Mirror dinghy, can be sailed either as singlehanded dinghies or as two-man ones; some, again like the Mirror, can be raced or pottered. Among the most popular singlehanded dinghies are the Laser and the Topper, both of which offer exciting racing for the experienced sailor.

Among what I have called dayboats there are older designs such as the Yachting World Dayboat, which are clinker built in wood and are raced keenly in some areas, and more recent ones such as the 16 ft Wayfarer and her smaller sister the Wanderer. The Wayfarer is widely used as an instructional boat at sailing schools (including the National Sailing Centre in Cowes) being relatively large and safe, but Wayfarers are also raced very competitively at some clubs. Harking back to a time of heavy wooden dayboats with massive iron centreplates, a modern dinghy with the appearance of yesteryear is the 12 ft Cormorant with a single gaff sail and a heavy glassfibre hull. She can well be sailed either singlehanded or with a crew and could be cruised with an over-the-boom tent.

Sailboards

With sailboards the choice is almost endless and thoroughly confusing. A beginner must seek advice from an established board shop as to specific marques of board, but in general it is better to begin with a flat board, which is one of high volume with a broad, fairly flat bottom. This gives it relative stability and makes the learning process a little less painful. More experienced boardsailors who have been through a series of lessons at an RYA recognized school may already have enough knowledge to select a board, but again it is as well to seek

Plate 1.4. *Boardsailing has become a major sport in its own right, attracting many participants who would otherwise never consider buying a boat. The relatively low cost of the boards coupled with the tremendous thrill of speed and oneness with the board, the wind and the water appeal to a wide range of people from the very young to the quite elderly, some wishing only to sail for pleasure, while others choose to race and others, like the man here, go in for ultimate speed. Whatever your aims with a board, it is wise to take lessons in the early stages from a qualified instructor.*

expert advice, particularly regarding categories of racing board as these are split into Division 1 and 2 boards and you need to know what you are getting into.

Any racing sailboard has a slimmer, more boat-shaped hull than a beginner's board and the refinements and details are difficult to describe. It is again sensible to go along with what is being raced at your chosen club at least until you have a better understanding and more experience to enable you to pick a board best suited to your weight, the sailing conditions and so on.

Higher up the scale you will find boards carrying foot straps which become invaluable if you take up wave jumping. Also the boards change shape and size, acquiring such striking names as pintails and 'sinkers'. These last literally sink if you try to stand up on them before they are moving, but once away they are very fast and are mainly used for speed sailing.

The majority of board buyers will go for a stock board of popular make that will take a few knocks, be easy to rig and give them a few hours fun when the sun shines and in that area it is a cheap and exciting branch of sailing. Indeed many people on family boats take a board along with them for use when at anchor in the evening.

Sailing cruisers

Here again there is a bewildering range of designs to choose from, each offering the potential buyer some of the things he wants, but probably not all of them. This is always the problem with buying a stock design; she will be a compromise. It is very unlikely that you will find your perfect boat, meeting all your hopes and desires, being built as a production class. It is tempting to say that the only way to achieve the perfect boat is to have her designed and built for you as a one-off, but even then you will probably have to make compromises for one requirement to blend in with another.

Don't dismay, however, of finding a boat that will meet the great majority of your needs and provide you with a thoroughly satisfactory purchase. That is one of the nice things about having such a wide range of designs available, there is one somewhere that will suit you, but you need to define fairly accurately what your needs are.

At the top of the market there are large, powerful cruisers

Plate 1.5. *A 26 ft weekend cruising catamaran that offers fast, fun sailing with basic overnight accommodation split between the two hulls. She could well be rather wet to sail upwind, but doubtless would give many people the taste for the excitement of lightweight multihull sailing.*

that would make fine homes for prolonged periods and that are perfectly capable of being cruised world-wide. More modestly there are the boats that provide a family with adequate accommodation, without too many frills, and that will allow them to cruise in safety both coastwise and on cross-Channel or North Sea passages in sensible weather conditions. Then, at the lower end of the range there are what could be classed as weekenders. These small cruisers have good overnight accommodation with all the necessities for cooking and sleeping, but which are rather too small for a family to spend prolonged periods aboard. They will be fine for estuary and short coastal hops but would not be chosen for longer cruises. Having thus defined three ranges of cruiser it is true that several tiny boats have made very extensive cruises in safety under competent captains and I have, like many others, cruised fairly widely in so-called weekenders, but any boat is best kept within her design limitations, both for the crew's safety and their comfort and enjoyment.

Which level of cruising you are interested in, together with

Plate 1.6. *A 20 ft lifting keel trailer sailer that was designed specifically as a trailer sailer and therefore has a tailored piggyback launching trolley and trailer assembly for easy launching and recovery. Fast and with good weekend accommodation the Medina, in common with others of similar type, can provide the family with good sailing wherever they can trail her to and launch her, besides offering the advantage of winter storage at home to reduce yard bills.*

your financial limitations, will initially dictate the kind and size of cruiser you should look for, but there is a further consideration in the kind of mooring you can obtain for the boat. If she is to be kept in a marina or on a deepwater mooring there is no problem, but if she will have to lie on a mooring that dries out on each tide you will have the additional factor of keel type to consider. Further, if you wish to take a small weekender from one cruising area to another by road, or simply want to store her in your garden during the winter to avoid yard charges, a proper trailer sailer should be considered.

The majority of modern designs have fin keels with separate spade or skeg rudders as standard, but are offered alternatively with bilge keels. A few are actually designed for bilge keels and an increasing number are being designed with lifting or swinging keels. The advantage of a bilge keeler on a drying mooring is that she will sit more or less upright between tides, whereas a fin keel boat will lie right over on her beam ends, making life aboard almost intolerable. Similarly a lifting or swinging keel cruiser with her keel up has very little draught and dries out very comfortably. These boats are also easier to launch and recover with a trailer as they require so little water to float in, even less than a bilge keeler. Their drawback is that the keel has to go up into the boat and can take up valuable accommodation space.

Motorsailers

In the last few years motorsailers have undergone a great transformation from being essentially motor boats with a bit of sail to boats capable of full performance under either sail or power. Indeed it is sometimes argued that most production family cruisers have such large engines, well able to drive them at maximum hull speed, that the motorsailer is a thing of the past. However, there is more to a motorsailer than full sail and a big engine.

Perhaps the main difference is that in a real motorsailer there is some form of wheelhouse or shelter for the helmsman and crew, which makes life for them much more pleasant in bad or wet weather. Such a protected helm station can lead to a false impression of the weather and a tour of the decks occasionally is no bad thing to keep you aware of what is really going on, but I can see many advantages in not having to sit outside getting soaked and cold if you don't have to.

Motorsailers used to be thought of as the province of the elderly and retired, but now there is an increased awareness of their comfort advantages among younger families. They not only give the crews a more protected and pleasant passage; their powerful engines ensure the ability to return to home base on a Sunday night in all but the worst conditions, perhaps under the command of only one parent while the other is looking after the children.

Of course one aspect of a motorsailer is the combined use of sails and engine, either through areas of light winds (or even calm) or in order to weather an important headland (for example) while on a coastal passage in stronger winds. Here their abilities under both sail and power are combined in a most useful fashion, the sails providing some drive and a lot of stability to ease the boat's motion, while the engine pushes her along nicely. Pretty much the best of both worlds.

Plate 1.7. *A pretty little cruiser racer that swept the board in her class at Cowes Week in 1984. She is a good example of the cruiser racer mix having not too extreme lines yet winning capabilities and the possibility of short term cruising by a light crew.*

Cruiser racers

These are all too often an in-between type of boat that can fail to meet the requirements of either a good cruiser or a good club racing boat. They have to be light and lively with a tunable rig to meet the racing owner's requirements, but they also have to provide accommodation for the cruising crew in addition to being simple enough for a family to sail without worrying over much about the intricacies of rig tuning. Thus, for example, where a true racing boat might have a small section mast with a pair of running backstays to control mast bend, this would be an undesirable arrangement for a cruising crew. Similarly, while it may be all right for a racing crew to sit up on the weather rail hour after hour, a family with young children simply cannot be expected to do the same. Thus there arises a conflict of interests.

In the end, the better designs tend to split into racers that are sometimes cruised, but whose owners normally use them round the buoys in a one-design club fleet, and fast cruisers that may take part once a year in the local race week. You decide which is likely to be your pattern of sailing and choose accordingly.

Motor cruisers

Like the other categories of boat we have been looking at, motor cruisers too have several sub-divisions. The broadest headings are planing, displacement and semi-displacement hulls. Planing hulls, like the sportsboats discussed earlier, are designed to run at speed on the after sections of the hull with much of the fore part out of the water or skimming its surface. Displacement types, like sailing cruisers, retain the whole hull in the water even at maximum speed, pushing their way through the waves. Semi-displacement hulls do not quite plane, but they do lift their bows more than displacement hulls and are thus potentially faster. Many pilot cutters are of this type.

Planing motor cruisers can make fast coastal passages in good weather but tend to use a lot of fuel, while displacement ones are much slower but use less fuel and semi-displacement hulls again fit in between. Displacement hulls are more seakindly than planing ones and are generally considered more seaworthy, although this may depend on the crew's boat handling skills.

For cruising on rivers and canals a planing hull is pointless as speed restrictions (and common sense) mean that they must

Plate 1.8. *Passing bags aboard a motor cruiser from an inflatable tender. The canvas bow dodger will help to keep spray out of the dinghy and an outboard can be mounted on the proper bracket fitted on the stern. Standing up and passing gear out like this must be done carefully as the soft bottom of the inflatable can move and throw you off balance. A boarding ladder would make climbing these high topsides easier, but note the section of guardrails removed for boarding.*

always be used at displacement speeds, so a displacement cruiser is the best choice and preferably one designed for rivers or canals. For example a canal cruiser for use on the British waterways needs a restricted beam of 6 ft 10 in to cope with the narrow locks, but can have vertical sides and rather square ends to offer maximum internal space.

If you are looking for an offshore cruiser, whether planing, displacement or semi-displacement you must consider the protection of the helmsman, the availability of a good chart space for navigation besides cooking facilities and accommodation – all in the same manner as the sailing cruiser buyer would.

Some motor cruisers designed for offshore work can have a short mast and steadying sail to ease the boat's rolling in a seaway. As an alternative to expensive and complicated hydraulic stabilizers this may be a good choice.

Tenders and dinghies

Tenders can be either rigid, folding or inflatable. A rigid dinghy can carry a lot of gear and is easy to row or drive with an outboard, but is difficult to bring on deck when making a long passage. They can be towed at sea but are difficult in rough water. A folding dinghy can offer many of the advantages of a rigid dinghy while being easily collapsed for stowage on board at sea. A good one, such as the Seahopper, takes only a couple of minutes to construct when required and makes a good tender. Inflatables are enormously popular as they can be deflated wholly or partially and easily stowed on deck or in a locker. It takes a while to blow them up again using a hand or foot pump and requires some available deck space, but they remain buoyant even if one compartment is punctured and will not damage a parent vessel's topsides when lying alongside. Adversely, they are very difficult to row in choppy water or against a strong headwind, having almost no grip on the water and usually short, stubby oars. Under outboard they can be rather wet. They can, however, be brought aboard easily, as already stated, and that is a tremendous advantage at sea. They have to be towed on a very tight line, otherwise they skid around astern and tend to flip over in a fresh breeze.

For sea angling a rigid boat is required that is of good size, is stable and has sufficient buoyancy incorporated to remain afloat even if swamped. They must have an adequate outboard and be capable of being rowed efficiently if necessary. Of course such safety gear as an adequate anchor and cable besides a pack of flares must be carried, but it is important to start with a safe boat. Many sea anglers go a long way out to sea in poor weather and at all times of day and night, so if they are to avoid getting into difficulties they must make sure their boats and equipment are up to scratch.

Hull materials and construction

The vast majority of production boats today are built from glass fibre (GRP – glass reinforced polyester). Boats are available in other materials, but generally they tend to be built in smaller quantities. Topper dinghies and many boards, made from thermoplastics, are the most obvious exceptions.

The fact that glassfibre is so widely used does not make it either an ideal or an infallible material. Its main area of fallibility seems to be in the development of osmotic blisters known as osmosis or (nastily) boatpox. These blisters that develop under the gelcoat can become so serious as to mean major surgery on the hull to effect a cure and neither their true cause nor a total preventative treatment are known. Having said that, it is an excellent material, being strong and requiring less maintenance than a wooden hull, for example, that has to be repainted each season. A glassfibre hull should only need painting after several years.

Apart from GRP there are several good construction methods including steel, aluminium and various forms of wood building. Steel is strong and durable but must be carefully protected from electrolytic destruction and is rather heavy. Aluminium needs careful working during the building process and must again be well protected against electrolysis, but it is light and durable and factually, if not aesthetically, requires no painting.

New wooden boats of traditional clinker (overlapping) or carvel (edge to edge) planked construction are rare today as they are expensive to build and need careful maintenance. They have life and natural warmth, however, that simply does not exist in any other type of hull. In more modern wooden construction methods, such as cold moulding or WEST, wood is often used in conjunction with epoxy resin glues to form a light and very strong hull by gluing together many layers of very thin veneers.

At the more exotic end of the market, in the one-off racing

yacht arena, there are many new materials such as carbon fibre, Kevlar, Nomex honeycomb and so on that cost a lot, save a lot of weight and are almost essential if you want to win races. I will say no more about them here as the likely owner of a boat incorporating these materials will have no need of a book like this, although the future may well see these materials in everyday use.

Kit boats

For many people buying a new boat is financially out of the question and instead of choosing to have a secondhand boat they set out to build a new boat, usually from a kit. Such a kit will leave a variable amount of work for the owner to do to complete the boat. Some require only a few fittings to be bolted on, while at the other end the hull and deck must be joined and the whole of the accommodation constructed as well as the deck equipment being fitted. Many builders supply kit boats with the hull and deck joined, the main internal bulkheads fitted, the keel on (and any other ballast fitted) and the rudder in place. This is

Plate 1.9. *Kit building, or the completion of a boat from her bare mouldings, is a popular way of saving money and spreading the necessary expenditure over a period of time. This display shows all that is needed to complete a kit cruiser with the least amount of boat building skill or experience.*

quite a good starting point as the owner already has what should be a structurally sound unit on which to base his work.

It is often possible to buy all the requisite bits and pieces to complete a kit boat from the builder. This can sometimes save a lot and sometimes costs a bit more than searching round individual equipment manufacturers, but it is certainly useful as you are then using components of a known standard that will fit and work and you end up with a boat that is more attractive to a future owner than one that has obviously been bodged up out of any old odds and ends.

This is one of the drawbacks to kit boat building: no matter how good you are and how well you finish the boat off, you can never sell her as anything but a home completed boat and that will probably reduce the resale value somewhat, even if you have produced a finished boat of a higher standard than a factory built one. The saving in cost at the building stage must be weighed against this fact.

Incidentally, when costing a kit boat project do remember that the prime saving is in labour costs. In other words you save money by *not* taking your time into account. The other advantage to home completion (apart from the satisfaction of a job well done) is that the cost can possibly be spread over a sufficiently long period of time not to require a loan with its attendant interest charges.

2. Where To Look

New or secondhand?

Once the decision to buy a boat has been made, whether she is to be brand new or 'secondhand' – which may, of course, mean anything from second to sixteenth hand – the problem arises of where to find the kind of boat you have settled on. Initially the best thing to do is examine the various yachting magazines dealing with your chosen aspect of the general sport of boating, since it is in these specialist magazines that the relevant boat builders, yacht brokers and private owners do most of their advertising. If you don't already read the relevant magazines on a regular basis, now is the time to start (even if it only means an afternoon in the local reference library).

Such advertising is split into two kinds – display and classified advertisements. Display ads are the province of boat builders or agents (particularly those dealing with imported boats) and equipment manufacturers and are the ones that use photographs, often in full colour, of their boats or gear and equipment. In other words they generally deal with new boats. The classified ads are the small ones, usually at the back of the magazine, where private owners run a few lines under a classification heading describing their boats and stating the asking price.

Whether you are after a new, secondhand or kit boat, it is worth studying both types of advertisements because the display ones will (or should) give you a certain amount of basic

Plate 2.1. *Crowds of people throng to every boat show. Many of them come just for a day out and a chance to dream; others already own boats and come to see what's new, particularly in the equipment line; some, the smallest proportion, actually come to buy a boat. From the serious boat buyer's point of view a show provides an excellent opportunity to compare one boat with another immediately, while all the details are fresh in the mind. It is also a good time to meet the builder and arrange a trial sail on the one or two boats on the final short list.*

information about the particular class or type of boat being advertised, while the classified ads may give you an idea of how that class holds their price and how readily available they are second hand. It will take some months to build up a true picture of availability and secondhand prices, but then the whole buying process is quite lengthy and at this stage time spent in studying, talking, discussing and generally gathering information is time well spent. In the case of a completely new design you won't be able to make such a comparison and must rely on your own judgement tempered by that of the magazine writers when they produce reports on their own trials with the boat.

When a particular class of boat catches your eye as a possible solution to your requirements, even if you intend eventually to buy a secondhand example of the design, it is worth contacting the builders or agents and asking for full details to be sent to you. Don't waste their time and money asking for brochures on boats that are not serious possibilities, but equally, don't hesitate to make enquiries about ones that are. Builders and agents realise that only a proportion of enquiries result in sales and will treat your request for information as seriously as any other; after all if you buy one of their boats second hand now and like her, you may come back for a new one later, perhaps even a bigger one, and your satisfaction may rub off on other potential customers.

After you have received details of the boat and have had time to study them, you may have a couple of queries about some details, again don't hesitate – provided that you are serious – to ring the builders or agents and ask your questions. The bigger yards have permanent sales staff available to answer just such calls. They will inevitably try to persuade you that their boat is the one for you, but accepting that (they do have a job to do) they can be very helpful. They know pretty well all of the competing boats on the market and should be able to tell you how and why they chose a particular method to overcome any problems that seem to you to have been approached by quite different paths on other boats. They can discuss options on gear and equipment such as engines and sails. A good firm, even if you come clean and admit that you are really looking for a secondhand boat, should still give you their time and help since public goodwill is all important in this industry and there's always a chance that one day you may want a new boat and then you will remember who was helpful and who was not. Don't take advantage of them, but make the most of it; advice is all that you will get free. It's also possible that your purchase of a secondhand boat will allow that owner to buy one of their new boats and you may find also that the builder or agent runs a brokerage list for traded in boats of their own type so that they can in fact offer you the secondhand or new version of the boat you are interested in. It's worth asking.

Understanding advertisements

Though fewer abbreviations are used in classified ads today it is still necessary to learn some of the basic ones to understand just what is being said. Many of the manufacturers' or trade names will become familiar from looking through the display ads, so that when you see a boat listed as having 'six sails (Hood, North and Horizon)', you will recognise these as being the names of the sailmakers. Similarly you will soon come to realise that a boat with 'full B & G' is equipped with a range (though not always as complete as 'full' would have you think) of Brookes & Gatehouse electronic instruments, such as echosounder, log, wind speed and direction, radio direction finder and so on, or that a dinghy with 'Needlespar' has a mast and boom made by that firm.

In general it is fair to make certain assumptions if nothing is stated to the contrary: most modern sailing boats are bermudan sloops with Terylene or Dacron sails set on aluminium anodized alloy spars. Also the majority of smaller boats are tiller steered.

If, at the beginning of a classified ad it says, E7963, N1480, OK 1671, Laser 59895 or some such abbreviation and number, it is referring to the class of dinghy and her sail number. These examples, are, in order, an Enterprise, a National 12, an OK dinghy and a Laser, but there are innumerable dinghy classes, so a full list is impossible. Most, fortunately, have names such as Fireball or Cherub so identification in ads is easier, besides which you will have discovered most of the relevant ones in the course of your studies concerning locally raced classes.

In Appendix A there is a list of common terms and abbreviations used in classified boat ads.

Going to a broker

Yacht brokers do not normally deal with dinghies or ski boats, but for larger sailing and motor boats they can be a most effective way of seeking out and buying a boat of the type you are after. One very useful facet of going to a broker if you are not completely sure of your requirements is that you can use him as something of a sounding board to bounce your ideas off. He is well acquainted with the problems of choosing a suitable boat and should be able to give you a lot of constructive help and advice.

A few of the larger brokers deal with boats not only all over the country but all over the world; however, the majority of brokers are smaller concerns concentrating their efforts on a particular locality or occasionally a certain type of craft such as multihulls. This cuts both ways: it does mean that you have to chase brokers all over the place if you want to spread the net wide, but on the other hand it does also mean that you can go to a local man and know that he will produce boats that do not entail too much expensive travelling to view and ultimately can be brought to your home port without great difficulty or cost.

Brokers are in the business of selling boats and they will therefore go to some trouble to help you if they think you are likely to buy through them. They also, assuming that they belong to such reputable organisations as the Yacht Brokers Designers and Surveyors Association or the Association of British Yacht Agents, have to adhere to strict codes of practice, carry good professional indemnity insurance and comply with the law in regard to trades description, consumer protection and so forth. They make their money by charging the vendor (the person selling the boat) a percentage (currently 8%) of the selling price; they do not charge you, the purchaser, however much work they have to do on your behalf and yet they save you a lot of paperwork and act as a useful buffer between yourself and the vendor.

We will say a bit more about the role of the broker in later chapters, but for the moment, so far as finding a boat is concerned, it is helpful to go and talk to a broker and discuss your hopes and aspirations with him. Once he has a clear idea of the kind of boat you are looking for and the amount of money you are prepared (able) to spend, he should be able to provide you with details of a few craft that are at least close to your ideal. Assuming that none of these is exactly what you want he will then put you on his mailing list and will send you details of possible boats as and when they come onto his books. Just like an estate agent really, and just like an estate agent he will send you details of boats whose asking prices are above your limit – no broker (or estate agent) ever seems to believe what you tell him about money!

Boatyards and marinas

A lot of boatyards and marinas run a brokerage section and usually have many of the boats on their books actually lying in their yard or in one of their berths ready for immediate inspection. This makes it very simple to take a quick look at what's available and to discuss the boats with the broker. On the other hand, smaller yards may have a few boats for sale without actually running a full brokerage service and may well know that one or two of their berth or mooring holders are considering selling their boats. With these yards there are always a lot of ifs, buts, maybes and mights, but they often come up with the right boat in the end.

If you go to the boatyard in the area you are hoping to keep the boat in eventually it is a good time to broach the subject of moorings. Even if they say you haven't a hope of getting one, at least you know. Usually, however, they are rather more positive; even if they can't fit you in themselves they can usually point you in the right direction for finding a berth.

Noticeboards

Clubhouse noticeboards often display a variety of cards advertising members' boats for sale and if you are a member of the club it is easy enough and often worthwhile keeping an eye on the board and perhaps even putting a 'wanted' card up there yourself. If you do not belong to the club you may have to ask permission to pop in for a look, but within reason nobody will mind, particularly if you are a member of another club, in which case you can normally sign the visitors' book, have a drink in the bar and perhaps talk with one or two of the members, enquiring if they know of any boats for sale that would meet your requirements. Putting the word about that you are in the market for a boat is always worthwhile.

Newsagents and confectioners often have noticeboards outside and sometimes these can prove useful, particularly when looking for a smaller boat, a tender, angling boats, sportsboats or small launches. Things like outboard motors too are often advertised and if you are in the market for one they may be cheaper here than elsewhere.

Chandlers also may provide noticeboards outside and again you will find everything from lifejackets and oilskins to quite large boats. Don't forget such noticeboards even after you have bought your boat if you require extra gear and equipment. If you are careful you can pick up some good stuff at reasonable prices, usually far below the cost of a new item.

Secondhand boat shows

There are now quite a number of secondhand boat shows dotted about the country and at various times of the year, notably the one at Moody's boatyard outside Southampton, which is timed to coincide with the Southampton Boat Show – there's even a bus service between the two venues.

These shows again allow the opportunity of seeing a number of boats at once, but you have to be careful to go through the proper buying process including surveys etc. and not just dive in.

Non-boating press

Exchange & Mart is a favourite source of boats and boating equipment of all types. At one time there were some real bargains to be had from its columns, but now it seems that owners are more aware of the true value of their boats and gear. Still, you will find the more unusual items that are not advertised elsewhere. If you need a tender this is always a good place to look, but beware when buying items of gear and equipment (and this applies wherever the private seller is found) that they are genuinely the vendor's property as there is a huge illegal market in stolen goods. It's a nasty fact that the steady trade in stolen boat gear often finds an outlet through advertisements in magazines and newspapers. This is no reflection on the publication as there is no possible way they can check the veracity of all advertisements, particularly classified ones; but it is something to be aware of because you stand to lose all title to the purchase if it turns out to have been stolen and there is no money-back guarantee.

Local newspapers too have sections of classified ads in which you may find a few boats for sale, particularly in papers covering a boating area. Just occasionally the large and expensive types of motor yacht are to be found in the columns of national newspapers, but these are not all that common.

Auctions

While it is possible to pick up a boat at a bargain price from a boat auction it is a risky business as you are buying 'as seen'. That is to say, with all faults. You do not usually have the chance to call in a surveyor to examine the boat's condition; all you can do is poke about as best you are able and bid accordingly. I would not recommend such a process to anyone who is a newcomer to boating and would advise caution for anyone who is not an experienced surveyor.

Word of mouth

Once you start looking for a boat, particularly if you belong to a boating club and mention the fact in the bar a couple of times, you may find that people will tell you of boats for sale, or indeed approach you as a possible buyer of their own boats. As with all boat buying you must be wary, particularly if the owner is a friend. Still, it's always worth keeping your ears open as a good boat can be sold very quickly and if you wait until she is advertised you may find someone else has slipped in and bought her. This probably happens more often with successful racing dinghies and yachts, but it's annoying if you miss out.

Boat shows

So far as new boats are concerned, boat shows are valuable to the potential buyer as he can see a variety of possible boats virtually next door to each other and make immediate comparisons, but they are not the place actually to sign on the dotted line unless you have made up your mind in advance. Shows are also useful for going round pricing up equipment, comparing one manufacturer's range with another.

I can never quite make up my mind whether I would rather

Plate 2.2. *One of the main attractions at the Southampton annual boat show is its floating section where boats can be seen in their natural environment. Being built like a marina with individual pontoon berths, this area allows the visitor to view and board the boats easily, while giving them an impression of what the boat is like when afloat. Here intense discussions are going on aboard a Freedom 33 cat ketch that, unusually for a boat of this size, has a radar scanner mounted on a tower above the pulpit.*

see a boat at a show in the water or out of it. In the water you can gain some idea of how she looks afloat in terms of appearance and trim, and also how she lies in harbour (stable, tender, lively motion), but out of the water you can have a good look at her underwater hull form, keel and rudder and how they are joined to the hull. I suppose it's six of one and half a dozen of the other.

Before going to a boat show try to decide what boats you want to have a look over and make a plan. On arrival go round making appointments where necessary as it is unfortunate that with the immense number of visitors to a top show it has become necessary for many companies to employ a 'viewing by appointment only' policy to avoid long queues.

Don't go round boat shows collecting brochures for the sake of collecting them, but if you are genuinely interested in a boat after seeing her 'in the flesh', be sure to get all the information that is available. Also, if you can, make a note of the name of the salesman you talked to so that if you want to find out anything

Plate 2.3. *Interested potential customers take a good look over a new cruiser at an annual boat show. Such shows provide the chance to examine several boats on a list of possibles without extensive travelling from one to the next.*

else you will know who to telephone or write to after the show is over.

Computer listings

There are one or two firms that operate computer data banks providing basic information on boats for sale together with the names and addresses of their owners or brokers. These firms do not act in the same way as a broker; they are more akin to a computer dating service in that they put you in touch and then leave it to you. An owner pays a flat fee for his boat to be put on the computer list and that's it. The firm does not take a percentage of the selling price nor do they act in the sale in any way. A prospective purchaser contacts the computer firm, specifies his requirements and is sent a list of possible boats together with the owners' names and addresses. Thereafter it becomes a private transaction in the same way as if the purchaser had seen a classified ad or heard about the boat by word of mouth. The computer firm takes no further part in the deal and has probably never even seen the boat. Your requirements may also be given to brokers that have listings on the computer so you may be sent details by a broker you have never heard of based hundreds of miles away: it spreads your net widely.

3. Inspections and Surveys

As it obviously costs a great deal of money to have a full scale survey carried out on a boat it is as well to make as close an examination as possible of a likely secondhand (or new) boat for yourself before calling in the surveyor. You may ultimately be proved wrong, but you should be confident in your own mind that you have found the boat you want to buy before bringing in the surveyor. Having said that, though, if there are a couple of boats that you are having difficulty choosing between, contact your chosen surveyor and discuss it with him. You can always ask him to carry out a preliminary survey on each of them and report back before beginning on a full survey of one of them.

The following remarks will be directed towards secondhand boats, but much of it applies equally to the purchase or rather inspection of new boats, which need the attentions of a surveyor just as much as a secondhand boat.

The overall picture

Gaining an overall impression of a boat is inevitably and sensibly the first thing to do. The old, old adage that if a boat looks right she probably is, still holds true within the limitations of the designer's intentions. That is to say a boat designed for trailer sailing is not going to 'look right' for ocean cruising, so you need to put on your trailer sailing tinted spectacles to view her correctly and in that case if she then looks right, she probably is.

It is not always easy within the confines of a boatyard, but if you can, stand back and simply look at the boat. Does she give the immediate impression of having been looked after? Are the topsides clean if not actually polished? Is the woodwork scrubbed or varnished? Is there a sign of water staining under the varnish, hinting of a cover up? Does she appeal to your eye?

That last point is not such a daft question. What joy is there in owning the perfect boat for your purposes if she looks like the back of a bus? Owning a boat is supposed to be a pleasure and there is aesthetic pleasure in seeing your boat and being able to think (proudly) 'that's mine' and that entails a sweet appearance.

The hull

Perhaps the obvious place to begin your closer inspection is with the hull. Assuming it is made of glassfibre, the first two things to look for are bad scuffing, scoring or abrasion that has broken through the gelcoat, allowing water to reach the fibres (along which water can travel by capillary action) and requiring quite a lot of expensive work to put right; and secondly, any signs of osmotic blistering.

Osmosis or, more crudely, 'boatpox', has long been recognized as the bane of glassfibre hulls, but still the cause and true nature of the problem is not fully understood. Exactly why one of two apparently identical hulls should suffer extensive blistering while the other shows no signs throughout its life is hard to explain, but some weight is given to the theory that the actual mixing of the resin and accelerator at the laminating stage can be instrumental in causing or preventing the problem. Anyway, provided it is caught in time for treatment it need not be a fatal affliction.

The common treatment for osmosis is the grinding or sandblasting of the affected area, usually the entire underwater surface, and then recoating by building up layers of epoxy or polyurethane. Consequently it is felt that if epoxy resins are used in the construction of the hull the risks are reduced (although the hull will cost more) or if the hull is painted with an epoxy paint prior to antifouling it will be better protected. This painting definitely seems to be worth doing, particularly as the cost and effort involved will be far less than the costs and effort involved with any repair work if osmotic blisters appear. A

Plate 3.1. *What the surveyor found. The bottom of this boat was riddled with osmotic blistering and is in the process of having the whole underside sand blasted to remove the gelcoat and all the blistering before the hull is refinished with epoxy fillers and paint. After treatment the boat was certainly as good as new, if not actually better than new, but the operation was very costly and meant a heavy renegotiation of the selling price. However, if the surveyor had not been called in before the purchaser paid over all his money it would have been a disaster for him and goes to show the importance of having a proper survey carried out.*

move towards the use of isophthalic polyester resins for the gelcoat rather than the earlier orthophthalic resins is believed to have reduced the problem and indeed the use of iso resins is stipulated by Lloyd's for any hull on which they are asked to issue a certificate.

Inspect closely the joint between hull and keel(s) and hull and skeg for any signs of cracking or over use of fillers. There should be a fair, clean meeting showing that care was taken in the original marrying up and that subsequently the joints have not been seriously strained. There should, of course, be no misalignment between keel and rudder.

Although the antifouling on a boat that lives afloat normally, may be worn away to the hull in patches, particularly if the hull has been cleaned with a pressure spray on being lifted out of the water, these patches of bare hull should not be extensive as they would indicate poor adhesion between the paint and the hull, perhaps due to some of the mould release agent having been left on at the time of original antifouling. In fact if the hull was cleaned properly, undercoated and then antifouled there should be no bare patches.

If the boat has a propeller supported by a bracket fitted under the hull inspect both the state of the propeller blades and the security of the bracket. It certainly should not be loose and the propeller blades should not be badly chipped or bent as this will cause imbalance and create vibration problems. If there are zinc sacrificial anodes fitted (lumps of metal bolted on and wired to engines and electronics to prevent prop shafts and underwater fittings being eaten away by electrolysis) check what state they are in. If they are significantly eaten away enquire when they were last changed.

Look over the rudder hangings if it is a transom hung rudder and see if there are any signs of stress or strain. Check that the rudder moves easily but is not sloppy on its hangings.

Stand alternately at bow and stern and look along the hull to see how fair it is. There should be no bumps where bulkheads are joined to the hull and hollows between them, nor should there be cracks or crazing of the gelcoat at bulkheads. A good thump with the side of your fist on the flat topsides near the bows will give you an idea of how stiff the panels are and whether they will flex too much as the boat pounds into a head sea.

Make sure that toerails have not been too badly bashed about and that the stanchions are securely fastened to the deck. There should be no cracks radiating from their mounts. If when you go below you are able to see the area under the stanchions, check that they are properly bolted through the deck and a good back up plate. Screws are not enough if a person falls against the guardrails.

Have a look at the state of the deck and see if the non-slip surface is reasonably effective. Does it need repainting or re-covering?

Look at corners – around the cockpit coamings, the cabin coachroof, hatches – and see if there are radiating cracks indicating stress problems. Ditto the cockpit sole. Is it very flexible, indicating rather light mouldings?

Lift cockpit lids and check the hinges and fastenings. Check the main hatch to see if it is cracked where someone has stepped on it.

All these things are quite quick to do, they can be done discreetly if you wish, but they will tell you a lot about the care or lack of attention given to the boat. Don't expect a boat that is a few seasons old to be immaculate, but she should be reasonable.

Interior

The interior of the boat should be clean and dry with a reasonably fresh smell. Any boat that has been shut up for a time will be a little 'dead' smelling, but if the ventilation has been adequate this should not be bad. Any signs of damp or mildew on bunk cushions, fungus on deckheads and so on are indicators of potential problems.

Look around for grabrails and posts in the right places and make sure that doors to cabins and lockers fit properly, fasten properly and are not warped. Crazing of the windows should be treated with suspicion and any opening ports should move freely and have good fastenings to keep them shut.

The galley and heads are give-away places. Both should be clean and fresh. The cooker should, if installed in gimbals, swing freely yet be lockable. The gas pipes should show no signs of wear and there should be easy access to the stop valves. Copper gas piping should be used with frequent fastenings, just having flexible pipe at the last stage to the gimballed cooker. Taps on the stove should click off properly requiring to be pushed in and turned to turn the gas on. Is there adequate locker space for food, cutlery and crockery? Do you have to reach right over the burners to get at the lockers?

The heads should again be clean and sweet. The pumps should not be rust and corrosion stained. They should operate freely and look as though they have been maintained. The pan and lid should be clean and not cracked and dirty. There should not be any nasty looking water sloshing about around the through hull gland and the seacocks should be easily reached and turn freely. It is not a bad idea to shut yourself in the heads just to see if there is adequate room. Similarly if there is a shower fitted think about how much space there is to use it. Same for a wash basin. These are sometimes so awkwardly placed, half under the sidedeck, that you can barely get at them without permanent damage to yourself.

Lockers for clothes should be clean and dry and look as though they are normally that way. They should have ventilation too.

The cabin table needs to be strong and if it is of the type that stands on a single pillar, it should not be too loose and sloppy. These are vulnerable if someone falls against them heavily.

Check that the berths are of adequate size and that you can get in and out of them fairly easily, particularly quarter berths or doubles that look clever on paper or in brochure pictures but are actually squeezed in under the cockpit.

As you climb into and out of the accommodation just check that the steps are all secure as a fall into the cabin can be nasty.

Engines

On any boat the engine should be reasonably clean and give the appearance of having been looked after. In a motor boat it should look 'used' but cared for. There should be evidence of cans of lubricating oil or two-stroke mixing oil. If an outboard is fitted there should be no signs of damage to the flexible fuel supply line if a remote tank is used and where the engine is small enough to have an integral tank there should be a proper filtered fuel funnel.

Can you get at the fuel tank and drain off the sludge trap? Is it awkward to get at the filler for refuelling? On a diesel engine provided with hand starting, can the decompressors be reached easily while swinging the starting handle? Indeed can the starting handle be turned without barking your knuckles?

If there is electric start, is the battery in good condition or are the terminals all corroded?

With an inboard engine try to see if there is a drip tray under it or does everything fall straight into the bilge? Is it very oily and dirty under the engine?

Does the power tilt mechanism work on the outboard or outdrive legs on fast powerboats? Are the throttle and gear shift within easy reach of the helm position? Is the starting key accessible but not vulnerable to being stepped on?

Sails

By this time you should be getting an overall picture of the boat and be either for her or against her. Assuming you are in favour so far, go on to ask to look at the sails if they are available, but don't do this if you are not happy as it is a waste of time unbagging them and repacking afterwards if you are not really serious. Your surveyor can look for you if you want to go ahead with the purchase.

However, assuming you are keen and want to see the sails, examine them for general wear and tear, staining or broken stitching and in the case of any using battens look for chafe at the ends of the pockets. Make sure cringles and hanks have not torn out and that the luff slides or bolt rope are not too damaged.

If by any chance a Mylar or Kevlar (generally a yellow colour) material has been used in the sail, check that it has not fatigued and broken where the sail has been creased. In fact it should not be creased.

Sails with a lot of staining and patching are obviously on their last legs and if they are coloured sails and have faded, you should be wary of ultra-violet degradation that will soon lead to the cloth tearing. The sun, particularly if the boat has been in the tropics or other very sunny areas, will quickly attack synthetic fibres if they are not covered up.

Gear and equipment

Following from that comment on ultra-violet on sails, check too that all the synthetic running rigging is of good quality as some cheap imported stuff does not include the proper inhibitors to protect them against degradation. All the running rigging should be in a reasonable state without serious chafe or damage. Some roughening of the outer fibres will do little to harm the ultimate strength, but too much will mean replacement.

The standing rigging and spars are harder to check as most boats have stainless steel wire rigging that shows little sign of damage before it simply parts. There should be no kinks in it and the bottlescrews must be straight. If they are at all bent they must be replaced.

All fittings on the spars must be secure and without corrosion. The fittings taking the shrouds and spreaders must be inspected for cracks or bending, but the surveyor will look carefully at all of this if they are accessible. Obviously if the mast is stepped it will be difficult for him to assess the state of the upper rigging unless he is able to go aloft.

Ground tackle (anchors and cables) need only a quick check to see that they exist and are adequate. If an anchor stock is bent it is no good, but beyond that you might as well leave this to the surveyor as by this stage you should have decided if you definitely don't want the boat and if you think you do, then the surveyor will have a more experienced eye to cast over these difficult items.

So far as electronic instruments go, you have a problem. Essentially they either work or they don't, and it is hard to test, say, a speedometer on dry land. However, again the surveyor may be able to assess them better and remember that if you are buying through a broker then there is a legal requirement that if the instruments (or anything else) are listed on the inventory they must work unless declared defective.

Surveys

By this stage you should have a picture of the state of the whole boat that will allow you a rational decision on whether this is the boat for you. If you think she is then it is time to make an offer 'subject to survey' and, if it is accepted, to call in the surveyor. His job is to do a more thorough inspection than you have and to report to you his findings. On the basis of these you either go ahead with the purchase, stop it or make a modified offer in the light of the additional cost you will have to bear to put right discovered defects. Remember though if you do this, that you cannot go back with a lower offer because the surveyor has found something wrong that you have already used as a bargaining point.

It is not uncommon for a survey to reveal a defect of which the owner was genuinely ignorant so don't immediately dub him a charlatan if your man turns up a problem. Equally, if something has been purposely hidden your surveyor may be wary of the whole boat. Remember too that he can only inspect what is available and what is accessible. In other words if the sails have been taken away he can not look them over and if the mast is stepped with no means of going aloft he cannot tell you the state of the masthead fittings, but having said that, a good surveyor, a member of the Yacht Brokers Designers and Surveyors Association (YBDSA), will carry professional indemnity insurance to cover himself in the event of a customer suing him for whatever reason, so if something is missed that he

Plate 3.2. *The surveyor at work. As explained in the text, it is sensible to make an offer on a boat 'subject to survey' and then to call in a qualified surveyor to examine the boat thoroughly and provide a written report on her condition. All sorts of things will be discovered, many of them not serious and often unknown to the vendor, but occasionally a major defect will be found and the buyer must come to a new agreement with the owner on price. In any case the cost of the survey will be worthwhile for peace of mind.*

should have found, you do have some recourse to law. It is a complicated process but it is there.

The YBDSA maintains a list of members and has a code of practice for its members together with an agreed scale of charges. It is worth going to a surveyor who is a member as you then have some assurance of his capability, professional status and you will be sure he does not overcharge. On this point it is of course worth finding a local surveyor to keep the travelling costs down. A list of members can be obtained from the YBDSA (see Appendix B), but the classified ads in yachting magazines often make it clear if a surveyor is a member. Incidentally, under their code of practice, a broker may only provide a list of qualified surveyors locally; he can not actually recommend any one in particular.

Once you have found a surveyor, talk to him about the boat

you want surveyed, explain your purposes in buying the boat and say if there is anything in particular you are not happy·about or want him to examine for you. Don't produce a long list of things you have looked at yourself, just say that you were not too happy about, say, a dent in the boom or ask his opinion of the condition of the propeller blades. In other words show that you have had a good look at the boat but don't try to teach him his job.

If the boat is afloat and you want the bottom inspected (and it certainly should be) you must be prepared to foot the bill for hauling her out and returning her to the water. Similarly if the boat is laid up ashore and you want the surveyor to undertake engine and machinery trials (normally excluded from his report) you will have to arrange slipping or craneage.

It is best, if you are serious about the boat, not to stint on costs at this stage, for the charges he makes to you can save you many times as much in repair bills. I was buying a boat once and thought she was quite sound having gone over her very carefully, but it took the surveyor to discover a massive structural defect that could have cost me an enormous amount to put right. It was a chastening experience to receive a phone call only an hour or so into the survey to say that he had stopped work as there seemed little point in continuing without my express permission. I thanked him and withdrew from the purchase.

The surveyor is on your side, but he has to cover himself against any comebacks, so the report he puts in to you will almost certainly sound as though the boat is a complete disaster on first reading. Just sit down and go through it again carefully, list the worst points and if necessary ring him and talk these over. He has seen a lot more boats than you have and will know more about their repair, so take his advice.

4. Buying a Small Boat

The actual problems that may be found in a small boat such as a sailing or outboard dinghy are little different from those on any larger yacht, but since you are unlikely to want to pay for a full professional survey you must tackle the job carefully and thoroughly yourself. This means beginning with a general look at the whole dinghy to see if it is roughly up to the standards you are looking for and that there are no major defects.

Racing dinghies

With class racing dinghies a study of the classified ads in the appropriate magazines should have given you a good idea of the average price asked related to the dinghy's age and this must be borne in mind. In other words you can not expect to pay a bottom price and get a fairly new, well maintained example of the class. What you *can* expect to do is pay an average price and get a dinghy that is in adequate condition or better with no more than superficial problems. So, keeping your price in mind, begin by inspecting the outside of the hull looking for score marks, scuffs and gouges. If there is anything that has completely broken through the gelcoat look carefully for any signs of separation or delamination where water has seeped along the fibres. If this has not happened and there are no radiating hairline cracks, then check carefully on the inside of the hull for any signs of damage and look along the outside to see if the hull has been distorted. If all of that is clear then you should be able to make a reasonable repair if you are both capable and prepared to do it. Where the damage is not extensive then there should be no great difficulty as you will only really be doing a filler job and not a complete cut out and rebuild.

Similar remarks can be aimed at a plywood hull, since

Plate 4.1. *The International 14 is one of the most sophisticated two man class racing dinghies. They are fast and very exciting to sail but require a lot of crew skill.*

although it should have been built using marine grade plywood (conforming to BS1088 and bearing a BSI Kitemark) a damaged outer veneer may indicate more extensive hidden damage requiring a panel being taken out and renewed. This probably will not be an impossible job but may be more than you are prepared to undertake yourself. It would have to be allowed for in any bargaining over the price if it has not already been taken into account by the vendor.

What you might term bruising of the outer veneer of plywood – that is, a dishlike indentation of only an inch or two in diameter – is quite common as the result of a boat to boat collision at the leeward mark or a knock in the dinghy park, that sort of thing. It is generally cosmetic rather than serious and being so small can readily be cleaned of paint, filled, rubbed down and painted over, but do examine carefully all round it, inside and out, to be sure the damage is only local.

The rules of any particular racing dinghy class will lay down stringent building requirements and total weights and it is fair to assume that if a dinghy you go to see has an in date racing certificate then she has been built in accordance with those rules and will not have any problems continuing to be measured within the rules. You should also not have to worry about the structural integrity provided that nothing has obviously been damaged, but do insist on seeing the measurement certificate and if any required additional weights have been recorded on it check they are still in place. There is no point in buying a boat to race if she will not pass measurement.

Two areas where problems may be found are the rudder and the centreboard. If a dinghy is regularly launched and recovered from a trolley off a beach it is not unusual for stones and grit to be forced up into the centreboard case causing damage, or for the rudder hangings to be strained.

Lift the rudder on and off making sure that the gudgeons and pintles line up or that a single rod pintle passes easily through. Look for any loosening of the holding screws (bolts) and on a glassfibre transom check for hairline stress cracks radiating from the fastenings. The kick-up rudders generally used should avoid these problems, but still take a look. Make sure at the same time that the rudder blade is straight and undamaged.

Going to the centreboard case, it may be difficult to examine

Plate 4.2. *The Fireball two man racing dinghy has a 'scow' hull with a small bow transom (a bit like a pram dinghy) that was originally designed for home construction. Most are now built professionally, but they still provide good racing and many are sailed by male and female crews, often with the woman on the trapeze wire.*

properly, but check the condition of the rubber fairing strips that are usually fitted. These form a seal over the opening when the plate is completely housed and all around it when the board is down. The strips are easily renewable if they are damaged, but such damage is indicative that stones and gravel may have worked their way up inside. If possible put the hull on its side and swing the plate in and out to feel if there is any problem and to check its straightness and condition. Look at the swivel bolt to see if it is damaged. This may mean withdrawing it, but that should not be difficult with the right tools and where a daggerboard (straight up and down, unpivoted) is used, check the after end of the hull opening to see if it has been cracked when the dinghy has run aground.

Take a look at the self-draining system on the dinghy and see that the bailers operate properly, particularly that they close and lock easily. It is embarrassing to launch your newly acquired dinghy only to have it start filling with water because the bailers won't shut – I know.

Leaving the outside of the hull, examine all the shroud plates, forestay fittings, cleats, sheet horse, fairleads and so on for any signs of stress or loose fixings. Anything that is bent should be viewed with suspicion. Check the buoyancy as far as you can for any damage or ingress of water. Look at the toe straps and their fastenings to make sure they are secure.

Go over the spars and rigging carefully looking for signs of wear or damage. Dents in spars are signs of problems to come as they form weak points. Make sure that spinnaker pole end fittings snap shut and slide open easily and positively. Make sure that the rigging is sound and that a trapeze (if fitted) is not about to part and drop the crew in the water. Spreaders must be straight and sound.

The running rigging should not be worn out and the sheaves and blocks through which it all runs must work smoothly. Check the operation of all control lines and see how much needs renewing.

Finally, if you are still keen on the boat examine all the sails for splits, tears, worn or broken stitching and general deterioration. Try to find out when they were last measured as a stretched or misshapen sail will neither give you good performance nor a clean bill of health next time you have to face a measurer.

Other sailing dinghies

The above has been directed at racing dinghies, but much the same can be said for any sort of sailing dinghy or dayboat. If the boat has a fixed keel you must check the keel bolts as best you can, probably finding out how old they are (which is likely to be the same age as the boat) and testing their tightness. Look under the boat at the hull to keel joint and see that it is tight and not shedding a lot of filler. Also look to see that keel and rudder are aligned properly.

If you are examining a camping or cruising dinghy give a lot of thought to the stowage of all the necessary gear and equipment, assuring yourself that there is adequate secure locker space where equipment will remain if the boat is capsized and will, in the course of normal sailing, be kept nice and dry. Some cruising dinghies will carry an outboard motor and obviously this must be checked over to see that its condition is reasonable and that it actually works. Check also that it can be stowed securely without leaking petrol or oil all over the bottom of the boat and that the fuel can is properly fastened down. Then, even if there is a good motor, make sure the oars are in good condition and that there are rowlocks tied to the boat. Also, if you can, try to make sure you can actually row the dinghy – does it mean unshipping the outboard engine, even unstepping the mast? This may only be discovered by going out for a trial sail, but it is important.

Tenders

Tenders always have a rough life and buying a secondhand one means buying one that will not look pristine. If that is realized, then there are some good bargains to be had on the secondhand market, but these do tend to be snapped up quickly.

Rigid tenders are normally either glassfibre or plywood but a few are made in other 'plastic' materials. In the 7 ft or 8 ft size they usually have a pram (flat) bow to increase internal space, while larger ones have a stem. Although rigid tenders are much better boats than inflatables or most folding dinghies to row, sail or use with an outboard, they do suffer the major disadvantage for a small cruiser of being very nearly impossible to carry on deck, which means that on passage they must be towed astern. This causes a lot of drag and in a rough following sea they ride up and either try to take great chunks out of the parent vessel's stern or may even attempt to climb aboard.

Inflatables at least solve this problem as they can be deflated and stowed in a locker or partially deflated and carried on deck, usually on the cabin top. In this way they can quickly be blown up and launched when required, although finding the deck space to do this is not always easy on a small cruiser. Never try to tow an inflatable at sea, and only with the bow hauled right up to deck level when in harbour as they flip over on a long painter or in a strong wind, and the drag when filled with water will probably tear the painter from its attachment point on the dinghy.

The process of inflating or completely deflating an inflatable on a small boat is either amusing or infuriating according to circumstances and mood, but it is never easy as the dinghy ideally needs to be laid on a flat surface – and there isn't one on a small boat. The other drawbacks to these tenders are the difficulty of handling them in strong winds, either under oars or outboard, and their limited size-for-size internal volume compared with a rigid tender. They will carry just as much in terms of weight, but not bulk because of the diameter of the inflation tubes. It is also a dampening certainty that if they do not have bottom boards you will get wet feet when you step aboard as the rain and/or spray will drain to the lowest point – your feet. However, an inflatable is kinder to topsides than all but very well fendered rigid dinghies.

One great advantage of an inflatable dinghy is that it is buoyant. If it is swamped or even if one tube is punctured, the crew will still be kept afloat, whereas if a rigid dinghy does not have sufficient built-in buoyancy it will sink, leaving the crew in trouble.

Folding dinghies are somewhat less popular than either rigid or inflatable ones, mainly because they were not highly developed by the time good inflatables came onto the market. Since that time few people have paid much attention to their design. There are a few good ones on the market, such as the Seahopper, which combine the stowing advantages of an inflatable with some of the handling and load-carrying characteristics of rigid dinghies, but not many.

Rigid dinghies

When it comes to looking over a secondhand glassfibre or plywood tender the comments earlier in this chapter regarding racing dinghies apply just as well, but remember that nobody

Plate 4.3. *An alternative to the rigid or inflatable tender is a folding one. Here the plywood dinghy can be put together in only a minute or two and becomes a fine rowing, sailing or outboard powered tender in which buoyancy bags can readily be installed under the thwarts. It folds down just as quickly and stows either on deck or against the guardrails, taking up far less space than a rigid dinghy and competing well with an inflatable. When erected the dinghy offers the handling and volume advantages of a rigid dinghy.*

looks after their tender as well as they should and it is likely that the gelcoat will be scuffed and scratched from being dragged over pebbly beaches and so on. These scratches, if they are not too serious, need only to be rubbed over with sandpaper or filled and sanded down, then the whole dinghy can be given a lick of paint and it will be transformed in no time. It really is remarkable what renovation can be done and even a hole can relatively easily be cut out, repaired and the dinghy brought back to a usable standard. Such repairs are far easier than they are on a bigger boat if only because access to the damaged area is generally far easier. Much the same applies to plywood dinghies since there again even cutting out and replacing a panel is not always the major job it seems.

The dinghy (whether glassfibre or plywood) should have plenty of built-in buoyancy, but most do not so you should consider fitting some either in the form of built-in tanks under the bow, stern and possibly centre thwarts, or the installation of inflatable buoyancy bags in these places. I suggest under the thwarts rather than along the sides of the dinghy only because that takes up space while under the thwarts is more or less dead space already. If buoyancy is already included try to check that it is sound and does not let water in or that the bags do hold air.

It is most useful to have two rowing positions in a tender: one in the normal centre position, for use when you are in the boat alone or with two others (one sat in the bows and the other in the stern), and one in the bows. This second position is used when there are two of you, because with one in the bows rowing and the other in the stern, the boat is nicely balanced fore and aft, whereas if one person sits in the stern and the other rows from the centre, the boat will be down by the stern and very hard to control. So again, if a second rowing position up forward is not provided, think seriously about putting it in.

Still on the subject of rowing, it is nice to have a sculling notch or rowlock position in the transom so that if one oar should be lost you can still scull the dinghy. This skill can save you inconvenience and you may choose to scull even when

Plate 4.4. *Using a forward rowing position in a rigid plywood tender to keep the boat trimmed fore and aft. Additionally, this position leaves plenty of space amidships for baggage and other gear.*

you still have two oars available as it is a pleasant means of moving about.

There should be a reinforced, protective pad on the transom to take an outboard engine and if you have any intention of using one with an inflatable that has no wooden transom there must be a proper mounting bracket designed for that particular dinghy; it must fit correctly or else you will lose it and the outboard.

Inflatables

The examination of an inflatable dinghy needs to be done with it both inflated and deflated. It does not matter which condition you begin with, but let's take the inflated one first. Obviously it is important to discover whether the tanks hold their pressure or not, but beyond that make a careful examination to see if the fabric has been exposed by abrasion on any surface and check round all the seams very carefully for any areas needing

Plate 4.5. *With an inflatable tender there is only one rowing position, which means a passenger must sit in the stern and oars will bash knees, while the space forward for bags is not very great due to the necessarily wide diameter inflatable tubes making up the dinghy. Although the rigid tender shown elsewhere should have some buoyancy fitted, the extra space and ease of rowing a rigid dinghy can be seen.*

regluing. There are renovation kits available that contain glue and flexible paint for recoating old inflatables and by all accounts these are successful if used properly, so much can be done on the restoration front.

With the boat deflated you can more easily examine the joints between bottom and tubes, looking again for anything coming unstuck. This area traps grit and sand when the boat is in use and trouble often occurs here. Take the opportunity too of checking the valves and try inflating the dinghy to see if the pump works well enough.

Look over the oars, rowlocks, bailers, anchors and any other equipment for any obvious problems, particularly splits or cracks in the oars and make sure the rowlocks fit properly into their sockets and that the oars in turn fit into the rowlocks. Yes, you would be surprised how often people who use only an outboard have replaced a lost rowlock with one that is the wrong size.

Sailboards

Looking over a secondhand sailboard is little different from any other dinghy in terms of trying to find any serious hull damage and determining whether scratches and scrapes can be repaired satisfactorily. The skeg is often rather vulnerable and should be checked over making sure at the same time that the area of the hull round it is not damaged. Similarly the centreboard or daggerboard. Make sure it is not too battered and that the slot is not damaged. Try pushing it up and down to make sure movement is free and easy but that it locks in place if it is of that type.

The universal joint is the other vital item to check, making sure that it still locks properly into its hole or slot, but also that it can be removed readily. Neither a new daggerboard nor a new universal joint is all that expensive, but there should be no need to buy a secondhand board where it needs replacing as there are so many used boards on the market that you need only move onto the next available one. The choice is enormous.

Go over the mast and wishbone looking for damage. There must be no cracks, bends or dents and the outhaul cleat must be in good condition. The sail too needs to be examined for wear and tear, particularly chafed seams where they may have rubbed on the wishbone or the daggerboard when the rig has been laid down. If there are battens the pockets will need checking for chafe and at the same time the mast sleeve should be gone over carefully to make sure it has not been torn when the mast has been pushed in.

5. Motor Cruisers and Powerboats

Like any other type of boat, motor cruisers and powerboats are designed with specific uses in mind and cannot often give a satisfactory performance in another role. There is, as an extreme example, no way that a displacement motor cruiser will make a good boat for towing skiers. It may be possible to combine roles, using a planing cruiser for occasional waterskiing, but it is always better to have the right kind of boat for your purposes.

Motor cruisers fall into several categories according to design intention: sea-going cruisers, river cruisers, canal cruisers. From there sea-going cruisers can be divided into displacement, semi-displacement and planing types. River cruisers are often beamier than canal cruisers because canal boats are restricted to a beam of 6 ft 10 in by the need to pass through the narrow locks used on the waterways and although they can use more power than their canal sisters river boats do not need such large engines as sea-going cruisers.

Sea-going motor cruisers

Amongst the sea-going motor cruisers, the choice between displacement, semi-displacement and planing types depends as much upon personal preference as on how much you are prepared to pay. Displacement hulls sit firmly in the water right up to full hull speed, while semi-displacement ones lift their bows somewhat at speed and planing hulls ride right up onto their bow wave, planing on the boat's after sections. This

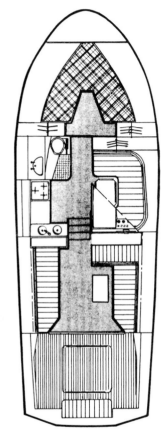

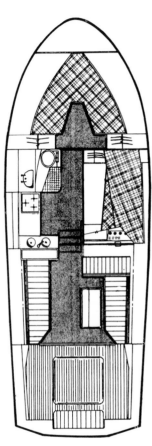

STANDARD ARRANGEMENT

OPTIONAL STARBOARD CABIN ARRANGEMENT

Alternative interior arrangements on the Princess 33 power cruiser. In the standard arrangement there is a dinette opposite the galley, while in the optional version the dinette becomes a two birth cabin and the coffee table in the wheelhouse (deck saloon) is swapped for a proper dining table.

performance naturally requires a relatively high engine power to boat weight (displacement) ratio and results in fast passages from port to port but rather high fuel bills, while a displacement or semi-displacement hull will take longer but use less fuel.

In harbour, the displacement hull will probably be most stable and comfortable to live in as the planing hull is naturally lighter, often with less depth of hull underwater to counterbalance the tophamper of cabin superstructure, flying bridge and so on, and can be rather livelier in her motion as other craft pass by creating wash, or when the wind gusts and catches her. This is not an absolute statement, but is generally the case.

The seakeeping qualities of the various hulls in bad weather depend a lot on the individual boat and the capabilities of her crew. All types of hull have survived gales at sea, but a lot of

Plate 5.1. *A 40 ft power cruiser with a flying bridge and radar tower. This particular boat bears the markings of being powered by Volvo Penta diesels and being used as a press boat for some offshore racing, but in other circumstances she would prove a good fast sea-going family cruiser. With both inside and flying bridge steering positions the helmsman can take his pick according to weather and the upper station certainly makes berthing manoeuvres much easier as there is a clear view of all four 'corners' of the boat.*

care and skilful helmsmanship is required to work (literally) a
planing boat through the high and breaking waves. Many
modern lifeboats of the RNLI are planing boats and they survive
the most dreadful conditions but they are in very skilled hands.
A planing boat has one advantage over her slower displacement
sister in that she may be able to outrun approaching bad
weather and make port before it strikes, but that will depend on
circumstances and warning time. However, what I am saying is
that it is not only the 'old fashioned' displacement cruiser that
will be a good sea boat, but she might be easier on a less
experienced crew.

High speed 'day cruisers' are like scaled down planing, sea-
going cruisers. They have accommodation that is fine for a
night or two but probably would not suit for a longer period.
They are in-between open sportsboats and full blown cruisers.
Some owners will use them for waterskiing while on a weekend
afloat, but they are not purpose designed for that. The
accommodation is limited, but like a small sailing cruiser, it is
surprising what can be fitted in and how much fun they can
provide.

River and canal cruisers

River and canal boats need much less power than sea-going
cruisers because they cannot travel quickly. In fact there is a
limit on the British inland waterways of a sedate 4 mph for the
very good reason that to travel any faster creates a wake that
will break down the banks. Over the years wash from passing
boats does immense damage to canal and river banks and it is
absolutely necessary to adhere to the speed limits to keep the
damage down and, when passing other moored craft, to prevent
them being damaged as they move against each other or against
their moorings.

The hull shape of canal and river boats is rather different from
that of sea-going boats as they must have shallow draught and it
helps to have vertical sides (topsides) for greater internal
volume and easier passage through locks. As the water level
falls the boat must not hook itself up on anything and flared
topsides will do this quite readily. The ideal shape for a canal
cruiser cannot really be defined, but certainly amongst the most
appropriate hull shapes are the miniature narrow boats
modelled on the old 70 ft cargo carriers that used to ply the

Plate 5.2. *A 50 ft steel narrowboat providing comfortable accommodation for six. This one belongs to a charter company based on the Oxford Canal, one of Britain's extensive network of narrow waterways that are no longer used for much commercial traffic but now provide a wonderful cruising ground for holidaymakers. Boats such as this one have their designs based on the old working boats with flat bottomed, vertical sided hulls for maximum internal volume on a shallow draught to take best advantage of the shallow canals and 7 ft wide locks.*

waterways in their heyday. These have vertical topsides, shallow draught with a flat bottom, tiller steering, an inboard engine and are often built of steel for durability.

The engine drive system on a river or canal cruiser may be quite different from that on a planing cruiser, which is often steered by the outdrives or outboard engines and has no rudder – not so good on a boat that has to be steered into a narrow lock at dead slow speed. A rudder makes life a great deal easier here, giving much better control at the low speeds and maintaining some control even when the engine is in neutral and not driving at all. With just an outboard or outdrive this is impossible.

Some river and canal cruisers are designed with a cockpit right forward and although I cannot actually say this is not a good plan, it is much easier to steer a boat from the stern where you can see the whole boat ahead of you. A motor boat of this type tends to turn about a point towards the bows and so the stern swings outwards. If you are at the stern this is no problem,

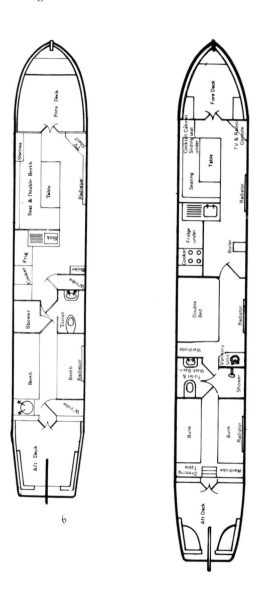

6

The 42 ft Red Rose is one of a range of narrowboats and is fairly typical of the kind of accommodation offered in a medium-sized canal cruiser. Being so narrow (6 ft 10 in beam), means that all the accommodation must be spread out fore and aft, so length becomes important for space. Even so, four berths are comfortably fitted in, although by moving up 8 ft to a 50 ft hull it is possible to have a permanent double berth in addition to a converting dinette.

but if you are at the bows you are unaware (or can be) of what the stern is doing behind you. It takes a bit of getting used to.

Because they are in and out of locks so often and always moor alongside something, canal and river boats should have sacrificial rubbing strips along the topsides – even if they are built of steel. Fenders can and should be used, but it is easy for them to be ripped off or to lift out of place as the boat drops in a lock, in which case the rubbing strips take the damage rather than the hull itself.

Features to look for

While a sea-going cruiser should have good guardrails round the deck they are completely out of place on a river or canal cruiser where they will always be in the way and are likely to be ripped off. Cabin top grabrails, however, are definitely needed on both kinds of boat, especially since the side decks on a canal boat tend to be extremely narrow to keep up the internal volume.

Plate 5.3. *Good engine access on any boat is vital for easy maintenance and troubleshooting. Here the diesel can be exposed almost entirely by removal of sound insulating panelling on either side, but even with just this one side taken away the vital parts can be reached. The one thing lacking here that it would be nice to see is a hand start facility.*

The accommodation on a motor cruiser, whether it is planing, displacement or semi-displacement, is obviously important as there must be enough berths to go round, the galley facilities and heads must be adequate and there must be such seemingly minor things as good grabrails for moving about down below at sea. The engine(s) must not intrude either physically or aurally into the accommodation beyond a certain degree. You cannot ignore them, particularly as you must have good access for maintenance, but on passage the noise must not be offensive and in harbour you want as much space below as you can find.

As a motor cruiser does not heel to the wind in the way that a sailing cruiser does, it may not seem necessary to do things like mounting the cooker in gimbals so that it remains upright while the boat moves round it, but this is not always so. Because of her faster speed the boat will move at times quite violently in any sort of a sea and then the gimbals are useful. It is useful too to be able to lock the gimbals in some fashion when in harbour, but even then there should also be proper fiddle rails round the top to keep pots on the burners should the wake of a passing boat rock your own suddenly.

Among the many safety features and items of equipment that can be installed on a motor boat an automatic engine-room fire extinguisher system and remote fuel shut-off valves are well worth considering. The fire extinguishers are fitted in the engine space and, rather like sprinkler systems in offices, shops and hotels, they operate automatically in the event of the engines catching fire. It is then vital to shut the fuel off immediately and you should not have to enter the engine space to do it, so a valve remote from the tank is desirable. You may have noticed that buses have them for the same reason.

Those are two safety aids normally left to the individual owner to worry about installing, but one thing that is often and very sensibly installed by the builder, is a warning system for any build-up of gases in the engine space, or an extractor fan. These operate when the engine ignition keys are switched on and you cannot start the engines until the fans have sucked the space free of fumes and the alarms have declared it safe. The alarms would sound if any build-up occurred while running.

Sportsboats and ski boats

Both of these types of craft most commonly have either vee bottomed hulls or cathedral hulls. When viewed head-on, the vee hull looks like a letter V and the cathedral hull looks like three Vs side by side or an inverted cathedral. The angle or steepness of the vee varies enormously from boat to boat but in all cases they are intended to give a softer ride through waves as the hull cuts into the water rather than slamming down on it as can happen with a flatter bottom. The triple hull is softer than a flat hull but because the water pushed out by the centre (deepest) vee is trapped by the outer ones the ride can be quite hard.

In both kinds of hull the after sections of the bottom are much flatter to give a planing surface on which the hull rides at full planing speeds when the bows are up on top of the bow wave and it is only the after parts of the boat that are in the water. The amount of flattening out again varies greatly and for example in a rigid bottom inflatable such as the Searider there is still a very steep vee right at the transom.

The depth of the transom also varies and this governs the need for either a long or standard shaft outboard engine. The difference is simply in the length of the drive leg between the motor and the propeller. If the motor is at the top of a high transom it needs an extended (long) shaft to reach the prop, which cannot be allowed to come out of the water when running normally.

In all sorts of sportsboat and ski boat the engine is best controlled by remote gear and throttle levers (often combined in one lever) by the steering wheel. It is not a good idea with such heavy and powerful motors to try to steer by hand on the engine itself. A wheel gives much greater and easier control and it only makes sense to have the engine controls to hand too.

The vee bottom boat tends to look vee shaped if seen from above, in contrast to a cathedral hull which tends towards the rectangular. This shape gives a greater internal volume for the same overall length and maximum beam, often allowing a forward seating area rather than just having seats behind the driver.

One thing to look for if you are going to be towing skiers regularly is a towing pillar in the boat rather than just a pair of hooks on the transom. The pillar raises the towline to keep it clear of the engine and maybe even passengers' heads, and if it is placed near the centre of the boat it eliminates the sideways pull on the stern of the boat when the skier flies off to one side. That pull, from hooks on the transom, can make steering very hard work.

Don't forget that if you are ever likely to be underway with your sportsboat or ski boat after sunset you will need proper navigation lights.

Finally, when choosing a boat for use either as a sportsboat or ski boat, you are very likely to have to tow it from home to the water and back each time. This means that the all-up weight (including the trailer) must be compatible with your car's engine capacity. The boat builder, trailer manufacturer and car dealer should all be able to help you with advice regarding trailing weights, but remember the legal top speed of 50 mph when towing, and to do that kind of speed you will need a good trailer in good condition with well greased bearings and sound tyres. If the wheels are immersed each time you launch or recover the boat, the bearings will need particular attention.

Outboards, inboards and outdrives

An outboard hangs on the transom outside and totally removable from the boat. An inboard is mounted within the boat and drives through a solid shaft through the bottom of the boat to the propeller or by hydraulic drive. An outdrive has the engine mounted inboard with a drive leg and propeller unit passing out through the transom, making it like an inboard/outboard combination.

Some boats can be fitted with and driven by any one of these units, while others are designed for one in particular. An outboard takes up no room in the boat, has a high power to weight ratio and can be tilted up for entering shallow water or reaching the propeller if there is a problem. Smaller outboards can readily be removed and taken to a repair engineer whereas an inboard or outdrive cannot. There is an indefinable limit to the size of cruiser that would have an outboard, but outboards are used on even the biggest racing powerboats.

Inboards can be worked on *in situ* without having the problem of leaning over the stern and dropping things in the water (you just drop them out of reach in the bilges under the engine instead!), but should you need outside assistance you will have to arrange for an engineer to go aboard the boat. Many people feel that they can look after an inboard better because they are familiar with car or lorry engines but I think that is really a psychological rather than a practical point. The underwater shaft and fixed propeller are rather vulnerable if the boat goes aground, but they do remain well immersed for good drive in all but the very worst sea conditions. A weed hatch must be fitted over the propeller on a canal cruiser to allow the removal of plastic bags and other rubbish that will be caught up.

With an outdrive this is not such a problem as the drive leg can be tilted up so the prop is out of the water; but they are not so suitable for canal or river use as they do the steering and entering a lock with no power on also means having little or no steering control. Outdrives are widely used on planing and semi-displacement sea-going motor cruisers to good effect as the engines can be pushed well back in the boat against the transom, thus leaving more of the boat free for accommodation. On the other hand this does put all the engine weight right in the stern, so the boat must be trimmed carefully fore and aft.

Ultimately, the power unit is likely to be dictated by the designer and builder without being a matter of choice, but you can always choose another boat with the unit you prefer. The main thing is to make sure that it is suitable for your purposes and that you can maintain it properly. This is vital on any motor boat as it is your sole means of propulsion and this fact alone is a very strong argument in favour of having twin engines or a small 'get you home' auxiliary – even a spare small outboard that can be put on in an emergency. It is not practical to have two engines in a canal cruiser and may not be in a river cruiser, but for anyone going to sea or into the estuary of a river some secondary means of propulsion is definitely a wise precaution.

6. Yachts and Motorsailers

Design trends

Great design changes have been made in the last few years to both sailing cruisers and motorsailers, bringing them nearer and nearer together until, in many cases, there is little to distinguish them, each providing full capabilities under either sail or power. There are still many motorsailers that are obviously motorsailers and similarly sailing cruisers that are sailing cruisers, but for the most part the distinctions are now subtle. Sailing cruisers have been given greater accommodation space without impaired sailing performance, and increased engine power to drive the boat at full hull speed even in poor conditions. Meanwhile motorsailers have been given improved performance with extra sail area and reduced superstructures, but have generally retained the idea of a sheltered helm station, usually in an enclosed wheelhouse.

This protection of the helmsman and usually the crew too, does make life more comfortable on a long windward slog or on a cold night passage. The addition of an outside steering position for use in good weather makes for just about the perfect combination. (I must be getting old, as comfort is attractive.)

The production of boats that sail well, motor well and motorsail well besides giving the crew a sheltered ride and comfortable on-board living, has resulted in a wider range of people being attracted to them. At the extremes they are popular with retired couples and young couples with small

Plate 6.1A. *The 26 ft Folkboat is one of the most popular traditional style cruising boats, offering simple accommodation in a seakindly hull with a full keel and transom hung rudder. Folkboats are also raced widely, originating in Scandinavia as a racing class, and although there are many wooden ones still in excellent condition, glassfibre ones are now being built that can be raced under the class rules boat for boat with wooden ones.*

children. For both groups there is a high degree of assurance
that they will be able to reach their planned destination
successfully together with equal alternatives of power that can
be called on according to conditions and manpower reserves.
All of this combined with easier modern sail handling systems
has made life far more pleasant and enjoyable for many boat
owners.

However, this near amalgamation of designs makes the
separate discussion of their features and considerations rather
difficult, so the following will cover both types, distinguishing
between them where possible or necessary.

The rig

The rig and sail plan of a cruiser or motorsailer must provide the
boat with sufficient power to drive her at good speed in all
conditions, but must be easily handled by small and sometimes
weak crews. Most production boats are sloop rigged but cutters
and ketches are also available. Few, if any, production boats
designed for family use are over-canvassed. However, not all

Plate 6.1B. *A Maxi 84 showing her expanded deck area providing increased accommodation space
and a comfortably large working/sitting/sunbathing area. This boat has a roller reefing genoa for easy
sail handling.*

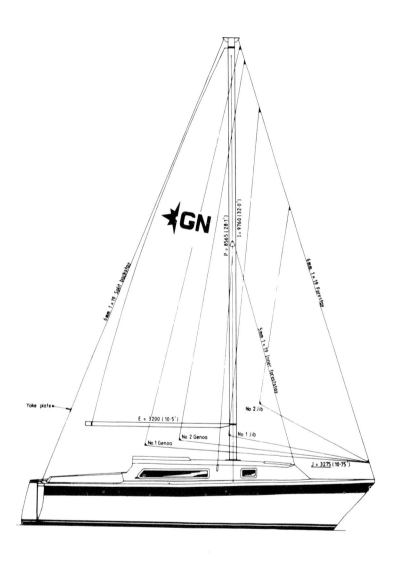

The *Westerly Griffon Club 26* is just one of the immensely popular range of Westerly family cruising boats but is typical of the general layout of most modern boats about her size. With a simple masthead rig and a possible six berths (although four people would have a much less crowded cruise) she is clean, simple and effective in design besides being enjoyable to sail.

such boats are arranged for easy, efficient sail handling.

Clearly no individual sail should be too big for easy handling and the way the sail area is split up is important. This becomes particularly true with headsails that have to be changed for larger or smaller ones as the wind drops away or fills in, the more so if they are hoisted in a headfoil so that they are completely unattached when dropped on deck. At least where they are hoisted with hanks securing their luffs to the forestay they do remain under some control.

With modern, sophisticated headsail roller reefing equipment many people have lost the urge to go onto the foredeck and make a sail change, preferring instead to rely on rolling up or unfurling the headsail. This involves having a well cut and well made sail so that it can work reasonably efficiently in anything from light airs to strong winds. A big light weather drifter and a small storm jib are useful to have in the sail locker, but otherwise these roller reefing headsails are good and have made the cruising life pleasanter. Also, having the one headsail permanently rigged (bent on) releases a lot of space that would otherwise be taken up with sail stowage and that is a nice bonus on smaller craft.

As with the headsail reefing gear, modern mainsail reefing systems have made great strides. The slab (or jiffy) reefing system and the roller reefing system, involving rolling the mainsail around the boom, are still the most popular, but the Hood Stoway system where the mainsail is rolled round a spar *within* either the mast or boom is now becoming widely and happily used.

Slab reefing requires the halyard to be eased, a cringle (metal ring) in the luff slipped over a hook on the boom, a similar cringle in the leech to be hauled down to the boom and held there by a leech pennant and the halyard to be retensioned. Just like that. If you want to tidy up the slab of sail it can be tied to the boom with reef points, but sailcloth today is strong enough if the sail is made for slab reefing not to require this.

As to roller reefing, this is achieved either with a handle on the side of the boom operating a worm drive to revolve the boom and roll up the sail while the halyard is eased, or a handle on the forward side of the mast operating directly on the boom. Both systems can work well, but the sail and boom must be

Plate 6.1C. *A 31 ft Westerly Longbow family cruising sloop with slab reefed main and small genoa drives powerfully on a close fetch. Her cockpit dodgers give some shelter to the crew while displaying her name clearly. The anchor is stowed on a stub bowsprit that keeps the foredeck clear yet leaves the anchor ready for immediate use. A lifebuoy is to hand on the pushpit beside the dinghy outboard in its sea-going stowage. A permanent boarding ladder on the stern makes boarding easier and in the event of a man overboard could prove vital. The white cylinder at the port spreader is a Firth Firdell radar reflector whose smooth casing protects against sail chafe on a run.*

matched, with the boom tapered to take up the fullness in the sail and so prevent the end drooping dangerously near the heads of the crew in the cockpit. This is something often overlooked and if you have sailing trials on a boat with roller reefing, do make sure the sail can be reefed right down and still keep the boom clear of heads.

The Stoway system involves specially made spars but is neat, effective and easy to use. Rolling the sail into one of the spars requires a carefully cut sail but avoids any possibility of boom droop and means that the sail can be left bent on yet protected from the elements.

Going down wind with a bermudan rig, it is almost essential for good progress to set a spinnaker and a lot of cruising folk do not like them as they are not easy to handle. Alternatives include booming out a headsail opposite the mainsail or setting a 'cruising chute' which is like a balloon headsail that does not hank on to the forestay but flies free. Like the spinnaker it is not too easy to handle in a rising wind. The solution for a spinnaker and a light crew it to use a Spi Squeezer, which is a sailcloth sock with a glassfibre trumpet-like bell mouth, into which the sail is swallowed from head to foot so that you are left handling a long sausage not a massive balloon of cloth.

A few production boats are designed with alternative rigs to the normal bermudan sloop, cutter or ketch. The most popular of these must be the Freedom rig, which involves unstayed masts and either two-part sails that wrap right round the mast and set between the arms of wishbone booms, or fully battened single-ply sails set in a conventional luff groove and on a conventional boom. To many observers these rigs still look odd, but they are efficient, very simple to handle and increasingly popular on a range of Freedom yachts from 21 ft to 70 ft.

The other unconventional rig with its exponents is the Chinese lugsail or junk rig. This too involves an unstayed mast and sets a fully battened sail, but this time using heavy battens, the balanced lugsail setting on one side of the mast. Bigger yachts may have two or three such sails. The delight with the Chinese rig is its extreme simplicity in reefing or making sail. All you do to reef is ease away the halyard. The weight of the yard and the battens collapses part of the sail onto the boom where it is confined by lazyjacks (like twin topping lifts) and controlled by the downward pull of the multipart mainsheet. Another line or two can be adjusted at leisure, but that's all that has to be done, and to set more sail it just has to be hoisted.

A lot of running rigging is required, and there are chafe problems with this rig. Many people think it looks odd, but once you have sailed with it you have to admire its simple handling qualities. To windward it is not as efficient as a bermudan rig, but off the wind it scores heavily due to its more rectangular shape as the entire sail is exposed to the wind.

Steering gear

Although tiller steering is the commonest form of steering on cruisers, many motorsailers have wheel steering, making it quite easy to offer two steering positions (one inside a wheelhouse and one in the cockpit). A tiller is the more sensitive system, generally speaking, but on larger yachts a wheel is an advantage in being lighter to use. However, where wheel steering is fitted there must be provision for an emergency tiller

Plate 6.2. 'Twiggy', a home built trimaran that successfully cruised from Australia to England (seen here in pouring rain off Cowes). With a crew of two she made swift passages in all weathers, demonstrating the potential of multihulls as fast cruisers. Unlike the catamaran which either has the accommodation split entirely between the two hulls or has some in each hull linked by an often cumbersome deck cabin between the two hulls, a trimaran has the accommodation confined entirely to the main hull. As this hull is narrower than an equivalent monohull, the accommodation is often severely limited.

to be installed and used, should anything go wrong with the wheel system.

Access for maintenance of the steering gear is important and if wires are employed they must run over large diameter sheaves to avoid kinking or jamming. Finally a word of warning about wheels: plain stainless steel wheels may look smart but they are incredibly cold on the hands in only slightly cold weather, such as during any night watch. A nice leather cover or a careful whipping with cord usually solves the problem.

Engines

Adding to the minimising of differences between sailing cruisers and motorsailers has been the increased power of engines being installed in production cruisers. Where once the engine was of a few horse power only, intended for use in and out of harbour or at sea in a flat calm, the engines installed today are not extreme in physical dimensions, but produce adequate power to achieve full hull speed in a wide range of conditions and making motorsailing practical. They have stopped being auxiliaries and become alternatives to sailing.

With the importance of their role so increased, the need for good installation and good maintenance has also been emphasized. If the engine is going to be in more frequent use it must be installed so as not to impinge on life aboard any more than is absolutely necessary. The installation must not intrude into the accommodation space any more than can be helped, but it must be arranged so that all the main points can be reached easily for regular maintenance. Some thought must also be given to the possibility of its having to be lifted out of the boat; you don't want to have to saw holes in the boat to do this. The engine must also be sound insulated so that when it is running the crew still finds it possible to sleep, hold a conversation and carry on a fairly normal routine. It cannot actually be silenced, but it can be well muffled with acoustic insulation material fixed on the inside of the engine casing.

What fuel – petrol or diesel?

Although there has been a tremendous swing towards the use of diesel engines, the choice between petrol and diesel is still a difficult one. The price of both fuels has risen and the difference between them is no longer so great as to offer a quick way of recovering the extra cost of the diesel engine itself, which still costs far more than its petrol counterpart. Also, despite the production of so-called lightweight diesels, these engines are still relatively heavy, which can of course be a problem in light displacement boats.

Diesel is undoubtedly a safer fuel to carry on a boat than petrol, but with a certain amount of care there is no reason why petrol should be inordinately dangerous. Many people maintain their own car engines and they will be able to look after petrol boat engines, which are generally marinized car engines anyway, far better than they could unfamiliar diesels. On the other hand, petrol engines rely heavily on electrics and in a marine environment, which is hostile to electrics, that is a great disadvantage.

It is also a strange fact that many people who would insist on a diesel inboard engine are perfectly happy to carry the supposedly dangerous petrol for a dinghy outboard in a decidedly dangerous old one-gallon oil can.

Comparison of reliability of the two types of engine is not easy as the usual cause of trouble with petrol engines, as already mentioned, is an electrical fault or incorrect petrol/oil mixture in a two-stroke engine, whereas the problems encountered with diesels are mainly air or dirt in the fuel lines. With good installations such problems are avoidable – or at least their occurrence can be greatly reduced – but it is up to you which you feel better able to cope with or, hopefully, prevent all together.

Outboards

An outboard engine is, of course, a possibility on smaller cruising yachts, but few over perhaps 25 ft will be fitted with them. Some of their merits have already been discussed, but we should look at the outboard engine installed in a cockpit well, which is an opening in the bottom of the boat, covered with a hatch when the engine is not being used, having high sides to some distance above the waterline and onto which the engine is clamped. When the engine is required the hatch is opened and the engine drive leg tilted down into the water. After use it is swung up again and the hatch closed to give a smooth water flow under the hull. The advantage of the outboard in a well is that it combines the good points of the motor unit with the depth of propeller immersion offered by a conventional inboard

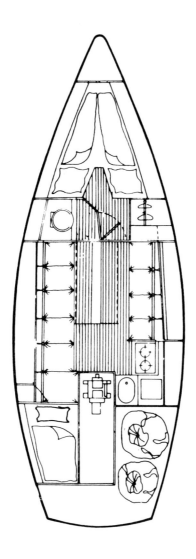

Interior of Westerly Griffon Club 26.

engine. Outboards invariably run on a petrol/oil mix and the fuel tank is normally separate and portable which makes re-fuelling simple and convenient.

Saildrive

One further arrangement that can be used with an inboard engine, but which takes up less space than the straight propeller shaft drive system is the Saildrive. This couples the engine to a drive leg, like that of an outdrive but going down through the bottom of the boat rather than out through the stern. It is a compact, space saving arrangement that is quick and easy to install, making it often cheaper than a conventional drive system. However, because the drive leg is fixed it must only be used where the keel will protect the leg; for example it cannot be used if it will project lower than a lifting keel.

Controls

Engine controls commonly consist of a single lever operating both the gear shift and the throttle, though some boats do have separate levers for throttle and gears within a single control unit. Whichever is used the controls must be sited in easy reach of the helmsman, but they must be protected from damage or accidental movement. In an open cockpit they can be recessed in a moulded alcove built into the side of a cockpit locker, preventing them from being trodden on or caught by sheets. Again you must check access to the back of the unit for maintenance.

Accommodation

Only in very few cases will the production boat builder make any substantial changes to the interior layout of his boats at a customer's request (and cost), so you are pretty much stuck with whatever is offered. This is not necessarily bad, but it does mean that you must consider the arrangement of comparable boats and see which layout you prefer. Apart from sleeping, the accommodation also has to offer reasonable cooking, eating and toilet facilities.

Berths

There will always be a number of berths that are more suited to use in harbour than at sea, including the ones in the forepeak at the point of greatest motion when going to windward, any without leecloths to hold the occupant in place, and double berths. As there will always be someone on watch during a

77

Plate 6.3. *The open plan galley and saloon arrangement in a 28 ft lifting keel cruiser. The keel houses in the white box with the tackle showing and, by careful designing, intrudes little into the cabin space, unlike the centreboard case on many older shoal water cruisers.*

passage there will usually be enough free berths for the crew off watch to choose ones that are safe and comfortable, but again it is something to think about.

The provision of lee cloths on all berths is almost essential. All they consist of is a wide strip of cloth (say about 2 ft or so) battened down along one side to the inboard edge of the bunk base under the cushion, with the free edge held up tight by lines from the two corners to cleats on the deckhead. This fabric wall then keeps the sleeper in his bunk on either tack, no matter what the boat's motion and when the bunk is empty it keeps the bedding from sliding out.

About the only bunk not needing leecloths is a quarter berth, which is a mattress in a tunnel between the cockpit well and the side of the hull. It is a snug retreat, often taken by the navigator as the chart table is usually by the head of this bunk, but it can be subject to doses of spray and rain coming through the main hatch if there is no spray shield provided.

Some larger boats have pilot berths on each or one side of the saloon outboard of the dinette. This berth, up under the deckhead, can be shut off with a curtain to allow someone to sleep there in the daytime if desired, but a leecloth is essential as it is a long way to fall out when the boat is heeled.

Most double berths seem to be made from the dinette by dropping the table down to fit between the seats or raising it to the deckhead and dropping in a seat back. Either way it is an in harbour berth for the most part although it may be possible to use the settee as a single berth on passage. Some larger yachts and motorsailers do have an owner's cabin in the stern with a proper double berth and some of these have a split mattress with a central leecloth to make partial use at sea possible.

What you need to do is count the number of people expected to be off watch at any time and try to ensure that they each have a bunk, with the full number of bunks being used only in harbour.

Cooking and eating

For eating, a dinette is now the commonest plan with a table standing between the U or L shaped arms of a settee. The old idea of a cabin table set amidships with settees on each side has mainly disappeared, perhaps because of the increased beam of modern boats, but in any case the dinette has the advantage of not obstructing the through passage fore and aft. It may, however, be a bit of a squeeze fitting everyone round the table. If the table does lower to form part of a double berth it is likely to be mounted on a single pillar and must therefore be treated with respect; the pillars used are strong in themselves, but a heavy man falling against the table can break it off the mounting.

Bottled butane or propane gas is the standard cooking installation on production boats with a cooker consisting of anything from a single burner through two burners and a grill to a full four burners, grill and oven, depending on the size of the boat. Whatever the case the cooker should be a marine one and it should be mounted on lockable gimbals with a protective crash bar across the front to prevent the cook falling against it if the boat lurches. Too few boats have this bar fitted as standard and similarly few provide a belt for the cook to lean against, freeing his or her hands to work. Most people would argue that both these safety features have their places only on larger yachts and motorsailers, but certainly the crash bar is important on all boats.

Plate 6.4. *The galley area on a 28-footer, showing just how much space can be achieved with careful design. The gas cooker offers two burners, grill and oven, while there are good work tops, a large sink and pressurized water supply. Notice the secure stowage for crockery under the side decks.*

Check that the gas bottle is stored in a locker that is ventilated and which drains overboard so that any escaping gas does not enter the bilges where it can build up to make a very dangerous explosive mixture with the air. This is the prime danger with gas on boats and must be prevented. To help it is a wise precaution always to turn the gas off at the bottle after use, but there is a reluctance to do so if the bottle is at the stern and it is raining. For these circumstances a shut off at the cooker (in addition to the cooker's own individual gas taps) should be provided and used. All piping must conform to the required British Standard with rigid copper piping and proper through bulkhead unions being used for long runs and flexible hosing only at the cooker (to allow it to gimbal) and the bottle so that the regulator can be moved from one bottle to another. In fact it is safer to use a downward spiral of copper piping onto the regulator.

Heads and toilet facilities

Privacy is very hard to achieve on a small boat and nowhere

more so than in the heads. Even if it can be shut off from the rest of the boat when in use, the toilet is much more a part of the living space than it is in a house and people have to adjust to that fact.

The usual arrangement is to have a heads compartment between the saloon and forecabin, generally with a hanging locker opposite so that the whole section can be shut off by doors to both cabins. The extra width so acquired goes a little way to compensating for the lack of elbow room fore and aft. Even so, using a wash basin can be a gymnastic feat if it is tucked under the side deck. A basin that pulls out on runners with flexible drain and water supply tubes solves some of the problem. Larger boats may have a shower installed in the same area; useful but again restricted in space.

An alternative location sometimes used for the heads is in a separate compartment to one side of the companionway. There is often more room here and of course passage fore and aft through the boat is not prevented when the loo is in use.

Whether a sea toilet evacuating directly into the sea, a chemical toilet with a holding tank fitted in the bilges or one incorporating a tank in the toilet itself, is chosen may depend on personal preference or outside regulations. Some areas do not permit the pumping of untreated effluent directly into the water, notably on the inland waterways, so it is necessary to check that the boat you are considering will meet the regulations of the area you propose to use her in.

However the toilet facilities are arranged, there must be good ventilation to avoid mould growing and unpleasant odours permeating through the boat. There must at least be one ventilator in the deckhead and an opening port helps. The whole area must of course be kept clean and fresh.

Chart tables

On a small cruiser it is nearly impossible to provide a permanent chart table, there simply is not enough room, but it is necessary to have some surface of adequate size to work on, whether this is the cabin table or a fold-out chart table. Such a device may be located at the head of a quarter berth or on a cabin bulkhead, but wherever it is, it must be possible to open out a chart and work on it comfortably; the small boat navigator's problems are quite sufficient without adding to them by providing a small, awkwardly placed table. Cabin tables are not ideal for the navigator, but are often better than a poorly designed chart table. At least the navigator should be able to sit comfortably and spread himself out.

Ideally, a chart table would be large enough to take an unfolded Admiralty chart, but on most boats it is more realistic to aim for one that accepts a folded chart, which is about half the full size. Electronic navigation aids round the table should not be positioned so low down that you have to pull the chart out from under them to work at the edges. Also, if the table has a lifting lid with chart stowage underneath, ensure that the hinges are flush with the surface and that the joint is as smooth as possible to avoid pencil points going through the chart as they pass over the hinges or joints.

There must be adequate shelving for storage of navigation books (almanacs, tide tables and so on) and also flat stowage for charts. Do not stow charts in a roll as they will then be impossible to keep flat on the table when you want to work on them.

If the chart table is by the hatchway it may be necessary to set up a spray screen to stop the charts and any electronic instruments getting wet.

Ground tackle

The ground tackle (anchors and cables) of even a small cruiser should include a main (bower) anchor and a kedge with at least 3 fathoms of chain and 20–30 fathoms of warp on each. If all chain scope is used for the bower then 15 fathoms may be sufficient for coastal cruising, but larger boats cruising deeper waters and going further afield will require proportionately larger anchors and maybe 5 fathoms of chain plus 50–60 fathoms of warp on the bower and 5 of chain with 30 of warp on the kedge.

All of this will need good secure stowage, either by keeping the anchor in deck chocks and the cable in a chain locker in the eyes of the boat or by having everything in a sufficiently large foredeck anchor well. In this case make sure the anchor can be lashed down to stop it jumping about and doing any damage, and also that the lid of the locker can be opened at anchor with the cable running between bow fairlead and mooring cleat. Remember in all cases to have the bitter end of the cable made fast where it is easily accessible.

Electronics

The sophistication and abundance of modern electronic aids is quite staggering. They include VHF radio, radio direction finders (RDF), wind speed and direction instruments, weather-fax machines (weather facsimile) and satnav (satellite navigation) units.

If you buy a secondhand boat the odds are that there will be several instruments already installed and these can be added to progressively if you wish. It is only if you are buying a new boat that you have to start from scratch.

It is hard to pick out what to recommend, but it would make sense to buy a radio direction finder and VHF radio before going in for course computers, Decca sets or anything like that. An echo sounder is one of the most useful of electronic aids as it can give a continuous readout of the depth of water you are sailing in, whereas a lead line allows only infrequent measurements.

Nothing comes cheaply, but if you want a totally integrated system linked to a computer you can have it, even allowing you to send telexes from on board; but what you have must be within the power capabilities of your ship's batteries.

Tenders

Inflatables are by far the commonest tenders, but rigid dinghies and folding ones have their advantages. They are often easier to handle under both oars and outboard engines, but they are not always so easy to stow on board and when undertaking any sort of passage it is definitely advisable to get the tender on board if at all possible. Large yachts fitted with davits on the stern can cope with any sort of dinghy, but for smaller craft it usually boils down to a rigid dinghy on deck chocks under the main boom, a folding dinghy flat on the cabin top or an inflatable either half deflated on the cabin top or fully deflated in a cockpit locker.

Fully deflating and stowing an inflatable in a locker does get it right out of the way, but hauling it out and getting it pumped up is not the easiest of jobs and takes time. If the dinghy can instead be carried on deck with either bow or stern sections deflated, it is quite easy to prepare for use. In fact in an emergency the dinghy could be thrown straight over and would support the crew while they completed its inflation in the water.

Plate 6.5. *A sound family cruising ketch on a gentle run when towing the dinghy on a short passage between harbours is just about reasonable. Notice, incidentally, the permanently mounted wheels on the dinghy for moving her about easily on land. Cockpit dodgers displaying the boat's name, companionway spray hood, stern boarding ladder, ready lifebuoys are all good features, as is the correctly mounted (catch rain position) radar reflector at the mizzen truck.*

Buoyancy in a rigid dinghy is important for safety as it is very easy to capsize or swamp a small, over-filled dinghy and many

such accidents happen each season, sometimes with fatal results.
For a fuller consideration of tenders, see Chapter 4.

Liferaft

Liferafts are expensive and require annual maintenance by a qualified service station. However, they are frequently real life savers and should be considered by the owner of any boat undertaking a coastal or offshore passage. Many owners choose to hire a liferaft for the duration of their long summer cruise, relying on their tender for the rest of the time. There are several arguments in favour of this, but if it is done, the tender must be well prepared and easily available in an emergency.

Leaving a yacht of any size and entering a liferaft must be a last resort as the liferaft is so much smaller and often less easily spotted by rescue craft. It must be large enough for the full crew (unless more than one liferaft is carried) and must be supplied with survival rations including water and a set of distress flares.

One drawback to liferafts is that they can only drift. They are extremely hard to propel or direct. An alternative that many

Plate 6.6. *The Tinker Tramp inflatable tender set up as a lifeboat with inflatable canopy for protection of her occupants. As an alternative to a liferaft these dinghies have a lot of good points including the saving in cost over having to buy both a dinghy and a liferaft.*

people are turning to is the use of an inflatable dinghy with an inflatable canopy. This provides them with the necessary protection from the elements, but also allows them to attempt to make progress towards land or a shipping lane. Again it is a solution worth considering, particularly on smaller craft with limited budgets and limited stowage space.

Motorsailers — particular features

As already discussed, the dividing line between cruisers and motorsailers has become blurred and in many areas of their design and equipment there is virtually no difference. A quick run through the various topics discussed for cruisers will point out the areas of similarity and variance.

The rig

A motorsailer's rig may be no different from that of a sailing cruiser of similar size, but in many cases a ketch rig is chosen to split the total sail area into easily manageable portions. Combining this with good headsail reefing gear and well planned roller or slab reefing systems for main and mizzen sails does indeed provide a good rig since it is often just right when motorsailing to lower the mainsail and simply have a headsail and mizzen set.

Steering positions

Frequently a motorsailer will have a sheltered steering position (often inside a wheelhouse) and an exposed one on deck or in a cockpit. This will mean having linked steering systems, probably to wheels, and duplicated engine controls. An outside steering position is nice on sunny sailing days as you can readily feel the wind and see the set of the sails, also it usually gives a better control position for berthing, but it is equally nice to be able to control the boat from inside some sort of shelter, even if not a full wheelhouse, when punching to windward on a cold, breezy day. The helmsman must be able to see the sails and if there is any major blockage of all round vision, the lookout must frequently go on deck to check all round for dangers.

As on any boat with wheel steering, there should be provision for an emergency tiller to be fitted directly onto the rudder stock with room for it to be used. A compass should be within sight too.

Engines

Here again the only real difference between the installations on a motorsailer and a sailing cruiser may be in capacity of engine and perhaps the space allowed for it. With more emphasis being put on the motoring capabilities of a motorsailer it is reasonable to expect at least a marginally more powerful engine, even though that in the equivalent sailing cruiser may well push her along at maximum hull speed in most conditions of wind and sea. Further, it is reasonable to expect a bit more working space round the engine. On some bigger motorsailers you may find an engine room approaching that of a motor cruiser, which makes access to the job in hand very much easier indeed.

Soundproofing of the engine space on a motorsailer is important as the engine is likely to be used more frequently and for longer periods of time. The engine must also run smoothly to keep annoying vibration to a minimum.

The greater expected use of the engine together with its likely larger size will mean that it requires more fuel per hour and so larger tanks will have to be fitted in. This will naturally take up space but is a price that has to be paid, particularly as motorsailers frequently carry more electrically powered items and so need greater battery charging capacity either from a main engine generator or a separate one.

Engine controls, like those on a sailing cruiser, may be either single lever or twin lever type, but may be duplicated if there is an inside and an outside steering position.

Accommodation

Again there will not necessarily be a lot of difference in the accommodation of a motorsailer and a similarly sized sailing cruiser. Occasionally, on smaller craft, there may be more headroom provided, but otherwise the considerations and requirements for the berths, galley, heads and chart space are all much the same.

Ground tackle

Here too the selection should follow sensible guidelines, but many motorsailers carry a foredeck anchor windlass where a sailing cruiser of the same size might not. Such a windlass is often a real boon and makes breaking out an anchor much easier. It may also allow the use of a larger anchor, particularly if it is to be stowed in the bow roller rather than lifted on board. If you intend using a chain and rope combination cable make sure that the gypsy on the windlass can cope with both. Also ensure that if the windlass is manually operated it can be done so easily and that if it is electrical that there is sufficient battery power available.

Tenders

Here again the choice of tender is likely to be dictated by deck space and the ability of the crew to lift a rigid dinghy on board. More motorsailers than sailing cruisers, however, are provided with davits on the stern for carrying the dinghy. This can be a convenient arrangement, but at sea the dinghy must be lashed securely in to the davits to prevent it swinging about; and in a big following sea it is possible for it to take on some water, so a method of draining it or pumping it out is useful. Otherwise the same arguments governing type and size apply as they do on any boat.

Safety equipment

The increased use of the engine and the extra fuel capacity on a motorsailer make automatic fire extinguishers in the engine space and remote shut off valves for the fuel supply wise precautions. Otherwise the choice of safety equipment on a motorsailer follows the same rules as that for a sailing cruiser of similar size, with lifejackets and harnesses for each of the crew, flares, fire extinguishers, liferafts and so on. It is largely commonsense but must be thought out carefully.

Club racers

In the areas of sails and rigging, the club racer does differ quite a lot from either a family cruiser or a motorsailer. The rig itself is likely to be more complex with a lighter section mast and boom capable of being bent at will. The rigging will be arranged to control the amount of spar bend and probably its location to make best use of the sophisticated sails the boat is likely to be carrying. The rig will not be as complex as that on a boat designed purely for racing as the club racer will have at least a nominal capacity for family sailing, but certainly it will require careful adjustment and some knowledge of what the various adjustments will do to sail shape and boat performance.

As a club racer is likely to be a one-design whose class rules will stipulate only limited variables for both rigging and sails, the sails carried are unlikely to be technologically advanced, but they will be much more sophisticated in their cut, materials and overall design than those production sails provided as standard

Plate 6.7. *The International J24 is a 24 ft racing keel boat that has limited accommodation and can therefore be used for overnight fast cruising. Despite being keelboats they can plane readily and have proved very exciting boats to sail.*

with production family cruisers, which are designed simply as good, middle of the road working sails. Increasingly such advanced materials as Mylar and Kevlar will be used in club racers' sails and they will require appropriately careful handling as they are expensive and have to be treated in exactly the right way.

The wardrobe of a club racer is also likely to be more extensive than that of the average family cruiser. They will carry mainsail, four or five headsails and a couple of spinnakers at least. Some larger yachts may carry more than this and as will be apparent, you are entering an area of great financial involvement if you go into racing with any spirit of determination to win.

Electronics

A wide range of electronic navigation aids is permissible on racing boats and, like the sail wardrobe, if you want to win you must have the best, so here is another big hole in your pocket.

There are restrictions on what can be used in racing and these should be checked before buying anything, but you will certainly require integrated systems for wind speed and direction, heading and log to provide VMG (speed made good to weather), accurate echo sounder, radio direction finder and possibly VHF radio as basic equipment with other kit going on board as and when you want it and can afford it. Before installing anything new, make sure you have the battery capacity to run it along with all the rest of the gadgets you have and always remember that it is perfectly possible to work without these instruments – they are only aids.

Rating certificate

Many club racers carry a full IOR (International Offshore Rule) rating certificate, but others need only their class certificate or a local handicap rating. It depends on the kind of racing and the particular club and class, but it is as well to find out what the form is before plunging into the purchase of a boat for local racing and then to ensure that when you purchase her she either carries a valid certificate or is sure to obtain one without much additional cost. Thereafter, keep it up to date as there can be few things more annoying (and silly) than to win a race on the water only to be protested out of first slot for not having a valid certificate.

Safety equipment

It may be that the club or class lays down rules regarding safety equipment to be carried on board or you may have to conform to the details laid down by the Offshore Racing Council for the kind of racing you are to take part in. This body, the ORC, is the governing body for IOR racing and lays down regulations for various categories of offshore race and these provide an excellent guide for any boat going offshore, whether she is racing or cruising. Remember though that they are minimum requirements.

7. Raising the Money

Boating is not a particularly cheap sport at any level and for most of us the purchase of a boat represents a heavy financial commitment. Some people are able to buy their boats outright from their savings but a far higher proportion require financial assistance in the form of some kind of loan to spread the purchase over a few years. There may be advantages in doing this even for those that can afford to buy from their savings as the purchase price of a boat is not the end of expenditure: there are moorings to pay for, insurance, storage in the winter, odds and ends of equipment to add or renew besides fuel and other costs arising through use of the boat.

It is these additional costs that can become a real financial headache if they are not planned for from the outset and it is because of them that a warning must be given against stretching yourself to the monetary limit when buying a boat. If you put everything into the purchase of the boat, the running costs may be such a burden that your enjoyment of the boat is impaired and that would make the whole purchase pointless. So do try to do the sums carefully before committing yourself.

There are several ways of 'raising the wind' to buy a boat and selecting the right one is not easy. In many instances of 'personal loans' the rate of interest you pay and the period of the loan will depend more on your own financial record than on the boat you are trying to buy. It won't always be so, but if you have proved yourself in the past by maintaining a steady job and repaying other loans successfully, you are more likely to get the loan you want at reasonable rates than if you have never borrowed any money before and are recently self-employed. In all cases it definitely pays to spend time (during your period of searching for the right boat) in shopping around for the best loan terms.

Getting advice

If you are likely to need to borrow more than about £5000 it will pay you to pay for professional advice and although a bank manager may be the obvious expert to go to, he will have an axe to grind in the sense that he is a potential lender and his bank will have a finance house attached to it in some way. Consequently it might be better to pay an accountant, whether you use one regularly or not, to look at your overall financial position (salary, mortgage, tax allowances, outstanding loans and so on) and advise you. If you are going to an accountant who is unfamiliar with your situation you must be able to provide him with all the relevant information for him to base his advice on and you must give him several quotations from finance companies to look at. In each case he will require, and you will want to know anyway, the APR, which is the Annual Percentage Rate of interest or the amount of interest you actually pay. It is a figure often quoted in smaller type than the 'come on' one.

When considering any loan offer you would be well advised to consider a number of points such as whether or not it includes automatic protection insurance to take care of the loan in the event of your death, illness or redundancy as the loan would still have to be repaid in any of these situations; if such cover is not included, check the cost of obtaining suitable insurance; enquire whether the loan company makes a 'setting up' charge or 'service' charge and if so how much it is; terms for pre-settlement in the event of your wanting (or needing) to sell the boat before the end of the loan period; finally if there is any possibility of the loan company (finance house, bank) calling in the loan early (foreclosing) and what you can do about it. If it all sounds a bit daunting then you would definitely be sensible to take professional advice as you will ultimately be signing a legal document and should be aware of exactly what you are committing yourself to.

Bank loans

Going to the bank for a loan is perhaps the most obvious source of money to most people requiring a relatively small sum (say under £5000), but the terms your bank manager will offer you will depend greatly on your previous loan record and general financial standing with the bank. If you have never borrowed from them before and can offer little in the way of security against the loan you may be in for a poor offer, whereas someone who has frequently taken out and repaid loans in the past may be able to negotiate a good APR, extend the normal five year term and push the loan limit up by a few thousand pounds. The fact that you want to buy a boat will be of much less interest to them than the fact that you want to borrow money; what you want to do with it may only be of passing interest. They would consider you in the same way if you wanted the money for a swimming pool in the garden.

It may be worth discussing a straightforward overdraft facility, but again the bank's terms will depend on your proven creditworthiness. One kind of automatic overdraft facility is that provided by the American Express Gold Card (or some bank equivalents), which may be obtained if you earn more than (currently) about £20000 a year. The card allows you an automatic overdraft of up to (again currently) £7500 at reasonable interest rates and over a flexible repayment period.

Marine mortgages

A marine mortgage from one of the finance houses requires the boat you are trying to purchase to be fully registered as a British ship under the Merchant Shipping Act of 1894 rather than the more recent Small Ships Register administered by the Royal Yachting Association. This is because the vessel is the finance house's collateral security for the loan and although the mortgage does not appear on the Certificate of Registry, it is recorded by the Registrar of British Ships at the port of registry and affords the finance company precedence over other claimants should you (the vessel's registered owner) fall into debt or be declared bankrupt.

In the case of a secondhand boat the finance company offering the mortgage will require a satisfactory survey report and is likely to offer only 75% of the price as against 80% for a new boat. Whatever the craft, the mortgage repayment period is normally 5 to 10 years although for large amounts this may be extended to as many as 15 years.

Interest is calculated and paid in one of two ways: first the capital is repaid in equal monthly instalments while interest is paid quarterly in arrears, calculated on the remaining capital at the beginning of the quarter at a rate of X% above the Finance House Base Rate (FHBR) or possibly Bank Base Rate, or alternatively, the company sets a notional base rate and you repay both capital and interest together in equal monthly instalments with the overall repayment period being adjusted to compensate for fluctuations in the actual FHBR or BBR.

The second method makes budgeting easier as there will be no shock interest bills at the end of a quarter, but will leave uncertainty about the amount of the loan actually outstanding when you want to sell the boat and also, although it may be paid off in less time than originally expected (if interest rates fall) it is more than likely to be extended (as interest rates rise). You literally pay your money and take your choice, but either you or your accountants must investigate such matters carefully together with what charges are levied if you decide to change your boat during the loan period.

Despite the boat being the real security for the mortgage company, your own credit history will be thoroughly investigated and will probably influence the actual mortgage terms offered to you.

Personal loans

Most banks are linked in some way to a finance house and if your bank manager cannot or does not want to give you a loan himself, he may well advise that you talk to the company he is linked with. Alternatively these companies are easily found from ads in boating magazines or attendance at any boat show. Like everyone else they will want to know your financial position and history before offering a loan, but if referred by your bank manager you may well get a good reception and favourable terms. Another way to good terms is by belonging to the RYA and approaching Lombard North Central who offer special rates to the Association's members.

In all cases a personal loan means a flat rate of interest with capital and interest being paid together in regular amounts, usually each month, and for a fixed term. The length of the repayment period varies as do the costs of insuring the loan against illness, redundancy or death and the penalties for early repayment (for example if you sell the boat during the term of the loan). Such matters need careful checking for comparison with the terms offered by each finance house that you approach.

How much you can (or wish) to borrow as a personal loan instead of going for a marine mortgage will vary according to personal circumstances, but usually the figures are around the £5000 mark with repayment being over three to five years.

Hire purchase

Hire purchase seems to be used relatively rarely and mainly for equipment or very small boats. It is expensive and you do not actually own the item bought until a (small) final settlement figure is paid at the end of the hire period – note *hire* not loan as you hire the purchased item from the finance company; you do not own it until you eventually buy it from them. People are not too keen on this scheme, it seems, preferring to go for a personal loan of some kind.

Partnerships and charter

The above are the main and common ways of raising finance to buy a boat, but it may be possible to find others, such as taking out a loan against a life assurance policy, but this should be entered into with extreme caution. Alternatively, you can consider the possibility of owning only part of a boat by going into a partnership with one or more other people. There are obviously pros and cons for such an arrangement, but those for whom it works advocate it strongly, although they almost all consider it wise if not essential to have a formal, legal agreement drawn up covering all eventualities of purchasing equipment for the boat, paying maintenance and running costs and selling the boat or one of the partners wanting to sell out.

Partnerships can work well in making full use of the boat if she is used alternate weekends by alternate partners or by providing a full crew complement if all the partners use the boat together. However, a degree of mutual tolerance is required as everyone has their own quirks and foibles and it will happen occasionally that things are not done or left in quite the manner you like. Also, although you only have to foot part of each bill that comes in, the desire for new equipment on the part of one person may come at a particularly awkward time, financially, for another. Tolerance and co-operation should get you through, but do go into a partnership with your eyes open and ask yourself the very pertinent, but non-financial, question: do you want to share your boat with anyone other than your own family?

Finally, you may be able to charter your boat through one of a number of companies that manage privately owned boats in order to recoup running costs, but if the boat is chartered successfully you may find yourself unable to use her when you want to, which would be very frustrating. You would also have to be prepared to face large insurance bills and higher maintenance and re-equipment costs as a good charter company will insist on a high standard of maintenance and outfitting. Still, it is one of the several ways of making boat ownership financially viable and as such bears study.

Making payment

At some stage in the boat buying process you are actually going to have to hand money over to the vendor, the broker or a finance house (in the case of a marine mortgage). I know that's obvious, but there are a variety of possible payment methods including suitcases of used notes, cheques, bankers' drafts or letters of credit and you must know what method you will use and be ready to use it.

The suitcase of used notes is not just a joke, people do actually turn up with suitcases of used notes and hand them over. Whether it is better to ask questions of such buyers or not is up to you, your conscience and how far away the nearest bank is. Aside from that, a personal cheque can take up to a week to be cleared from the time it is paid in at a bank, so that must be allowed for in timing the transaction, which includes paying a (probably) 10 per cent deposit. You will certainly not be able to take formal possession of the boat until the cheque has been cleared and for that reason, in some circumstances, it may be better to go for a bank cheque or bankers' draft. This is really just a cheque direct from your bank to the vendor, missing you out entirely (so far as he is concerned) and guaranteeing him payment. The cheque cannot be stopped.

A bankers' draft or a letter of credit may be the best method of paying for a boat bought in another country, unless you are working through a broker in your own country who will deal with the problem of transferring funds himself. If instead you are dealing directly with an owner in another country or with a foreign broker one of these methods will speed things up. It should be pointed out though that a letter of credit can be a very expensive item and your bank may advise a bankers' draft or a direct credit transfer to the vendor's bank. In this area particularly, your bank should be able to give you the advice you need.

8. Insurance

What is your cover?

Surprisingly, perhaps, there is no legal requirement for the owner of a boat to insure her, although a loan or finance company is likely to insist upon it, as may the organisers of any race you intend taking part in. However, with the cost of repairs and replacements as high as they are, to say nothing of the third party damages settlements meted out by courts in recent years, you would be extremely foolhardy to think of not taking out insurance on your boat even if nobody insisted on it. (Incidentally, the insurance company and you are the first and second 'parties' to an insurance contract; anyone suffering injury or any boat or other object damaged is the 'third party', hence damages as mentioned would be paid out under the third party cover section of the policy.)

Because insurance rates are (have to be) based on statistical surveys carried out by the insurance underwriters, there are types of boat, mooring places and sailing waters that carry higher or lower premiums than others. This may work for or against you, but is always there.

If you intend racing your sailing boat you will have to take out a policy that expressly provides 'racing risks' cover to the full value of your boat's spars, rigging and sails in case they are damaged or lost during a race; otherwise you may find, when making a claim, that they are either uninsured or only partly covered as many policies provide for payment of only two thirds value unless an extra premium is paid. Similarly, if you intend doing any singlehanded cruising or sailing, whether it is just a few hours or some weeks, check with your insurers to see that you are covered, because many policies will specifically exclude singlehanded use of the boat.

Using a broker

Although there is nothing to stop you approaching an insurance company directly, it is usually better to go through a broker as he can obtain quotations from several companies and so obtain the best rates and breadth of cover for your particular requirements. This is particularly so if you are seeking insurance for anything out of the ordinary, either an unusual, perhaps one off, boat or for an unusual voyage. The broker does not charge you for his services as he receives a commission from the company with whom the business is eventually placed and by going to him you can obtain immediate cover if the insurance requirements are straightforward. All it needs is a telephone call during which the broker gives you some quotations, one of which you accept, asking for cover to commence immediately. You are then held covered while a proposal form is despatched to you, which you fill in and return with the required premium.

By missing out the broker you would have to call several insurance companies, obtain quotations from them, then wait while the chosen company sent you a proposal form, which you would fill in and return with your money – and that all takes time if you are in a hurry to get the boat covered. Brokers are unlikely, of course, to recommend a club or class owners' association insurance scheme as he will not receive a commission on it, but do examine such policies carefully as some are good, but others are certainly not the cheapest way of insuring your boat.

Not all insurance companies offer a no claims bonus scheme, so check that too before signing up with any one company, as it can be a very useful way of fighting rising insurance costs.

If you are buying an old boat you may find that insurance companies will either not insure her or that they will insist on seeing a satisfactory survey report before deciding. There should be no problem about supplying such a report as you will want one yourself before going ahead with the purchase. Finance companies too may ask to see such a report and they will certainly insist on proof that the boat is comprehensively insured and that she is so covered throughout the period of their loan agreement.

Excess and value

When discussing insurance premiums with an insurance broker, the question of how much 'excess' you are prepared to carry will come up. By agreeing to pay a proportion of each claim you can reduce the premium required by various amounts. Usually the excess is based on a percentage of the boat's insured value: 0%, 5%, 10% or 15%. It is tempting to opt for the highest figure to keep your annual premium as low as possible, but remember that this amount must be paid by you no matter how large or small the claim, or indeed how frequently you make claims. If the excess you carry is too large it will make claiming a nonsense as it will either exceed the amount you want to claim or will be such a large proportion of it that it is not worth claiming and losing a no-claims bonus (if the particular policy contains such a scheme). It may also happen that you need to make several claims over a short period of time, which means paying out that excess on each occasion, so you must be certain that you could do so without bankrupting yourself.

The other temptation is to undervalue the boat to reduce the premium payable, but this only results in reduced payments being made in the event of a claim and that, combined with the excess you are having to pay, can leave you heavily out of pocket. Also, in the event of total loss, you would receive far less than you would need to replace the boat. Hence it is wise to value her as accurately as possible and to revalue her annually, erring if anything on the high side. You must not go too much over the top or the insurance company will rightly be suspicious of your motives and either refuse you cover or insist on a professional valuation. A modern and sensible trend is towards insuring, particularly gear and equipment, on a 'new for old' basis. In this case you value everything at replacement cost and if you make a claim, even for the theft (say) of a ten-year-old compass, you will be paid the insurance company's share of the cost of a new one of similar type. Such cover does cost more, but makes good sense if you can afford it.

Geographical limits

Before accepting insurance cover you should check carefully on

Plate 8.1. *When a really good insurance policy is vital. This glassfibre bilge keeler is believed to have parted her mooring in a gale and driven ashore on rocks that have battered her pretty well beyond repair. It's a terribly sad sight but does prove that even when safely tucked up in harbour a boat is always at risk, making insurance a vital expenditure.*

the exclusions and restrictions it involves; for example the case of singlehanded sailing mentioned above. The restrictions put on area are most important too, since 'UK coastal and inland' will be no good if you want to cruise on the far side of the North Sea (for example). Insurance companies are generally very good about extending area cover if given notice in advance and some will hold you temporarily covered if you stray beyond the normal limits through stress of weather, but do not push your luck with them, they would be well within their rights to turn round and say your policy is null and void. On the other hand there is no point in paying for world-wide cover if you intend using the boat mainly in coastal waters with just a once-a-season excursion abroad. Always cover the boat for normal usage and add any extension when required; it costs much less that way.

Calendar limits

Some insurance policies now allow for a period of twelve

months in commission to allow marina berth holders to go sailing at any time if the weather is suitable, while others still require a split of (say) seven months afloat and five laid up ashore. If that is the case, be sure you get the boat out in time or extend the cover. Particularly inland waterways craft could benefit from a flexible laid up/in commission period and sailing dinghy owners wanting to take part in winter frostbite series at the last moment should check with their insurers to see that it is all right.

Building cover

If you are building a boat either from scratch or from a kit, you might consider taking out a specially tailored builders' risks policy. The boat is clearly not going to be in commission for some time and at the beginning her value is substantially lower than it will be when she is finished. The risks involved during a building project are also rather different: transit damage, craning, fire, boat falling over or a car skidding into her, that sort of thing. Again you will have to search for the best cover available or get a broker to search for you and you will have to arrange for the cover to be altered and the value of the boat to be increased as time goes by and the building work progresses.

Transport cover

One thing to be very careful about when buying a boat is that you insure her specially for removal from her home port or builder's yard to her new home port. This may be done by land or sea and most boat transport or delivery companies will arrange cover for you if you ask them, but if you are delivering the boat yourself from outside your normal insurance area, be sure to get an extension for the duration of the movement.

Disclosing the facts

The different facets of marine insurance are legion and each case or situation is different, which is why you must try to get your policy tailored to your own needs and you will probably do best to go to a marine insurance broker. However, there still needs to be a high level of trust on both sides: the insurers have to trust you to provide them with all relevant information and you have to believe that they will keep their side of the bargain in the event of your having to make a claim. It usually works out all right, but, of course, if the insurers feel that you have withheld relevant information they will either refuse to make payment on a claim or delay it until they have investigated the case. Either way that is not good for you, so never try to keep down costs by not giving all the pertinent information as accurately as possible.

9. The Paperwork of Buying

Boat buying and selling has not escaped the modern desire for reams of paperwork and, as with any other major purchase, care must be taken when buying a boat to ensure that you understand all the papers you are signing and that you do in fact get all the necessary paperwork done. One of the nice things about buying a secondhand boat through a broker is that he will carry out all the form filling for you, leaving you to sign on the dotted line. Similarly a finance house offering you a marine mortgage will take care of much of the paperwork involved with re-registration and so on, taking a big burden off you.

Buying new

When buying a new boat it is likely that you will have to sign one of two types of contract with the builder, both written by the Ship and Boat Builders' National Federation (SBBNF). The 'Agreement for the Sale of a Stock Boat', applicable to series production boats, whether built in the UK or abroad, includes terms requiring a deposit of at least 10% of the total purchase price to be paid on signing the contract, with the balance to be paid within 14 days of completion. Particularly with boats built abroad this may be varied to something like 10% deposit, followed by 75% on notification of 'Factory Release' (meaning that the boat has been despatched from the builders) and a final 15% when you have actually accepted her. There will also be a detailed inventory schedule attached to the Agreement stating precisely what the customer is receiving for his money and that must be read very carefully before signing the Agreement. All payments will be subject to VAT at the current rate.

The alternative Agreement, used more frequently with one-off boats or customised boat construction is the 'Agreement for the Construction of a New Craft'. The terms of this contract include a deposit on signing of up to 30%, followed by a stage payment of another 30% on completion of hull and deck. A further 30% is paid when fitting out is more or less completed and the final 10% is paid after satisfactory 'Acceptance Trials'. Again all payments will be subject to VAT at the current rate.

These stage payments have been developed over the years as a protection for the buyer in the event of the builder's going bust during the the building of your boat. If such a thing should happen, you actually own the parts of the boat you have paid for and are entitled to remove them from the yard (or indeed to bring outside labour in to finish the boat) without fear of a Receiver holding them against the yard's debts.

The New Craft agreement can incorporate a standard 'Agreed Damages Clause' to cover delays in completion of the boat and it will also include a 'Satisfaction Note' for signature by you on completion of satisfactory acceptance trials. This Note, however, in no way limits your right under the 1979 Sale of Goods Act and in fact many builders feel that consumer rights are so well protected in law now that the Note is largely superfluous, but, since redress in the Small Claims Court is only for sums up to £500 and a full civil action would cost an enormous amount and take forever, it is most important from your point of view (as purchaser) to undertake as careful trials as possible. Indeed it is worth considering calling on the services of a surveyor to check over a new boat as you would have the weight of his authority on your side if any action were required.

If problems are found at any stage you must write to the builder (or dealer) in the first instance, setting out the trouble and requesting redress. Then, if that fails, write to the SBBNF (assuming the builder is a member) explaining the problems and asking for their help, for, although the SBBNF is basically on the builder's side, they do keep a close watch on standards and can suggest the appointment of a suitable arbitrator if necessary. Your solicitor may be able to help too, but if you are a member of the RYA it would probably be better first to talk to their solicitor as he will be better acquainted with the specific problems of boat building. Also, if you have taken out a loan for the purchase of the boat, contact the finance company who should be able to help you or at least give you sound advice.

Buying 'subject to survey'

When buying a secondhand boat it is always as well to make an offer on the boat you want 'subject to a satisfactory survey report'. This, if accepted by the person selling the boat, allows you to call in a qualified surveyor to examine the entire boat and report to you on what is wrong so that you can either confirm your offer and proceed with the purchase or renegotiate the price in the light of the surveyor's findings. You cannot, of course, make your initial offer, docking a few hundred pounds from the asking price 'because the rudder hangings need renewing', then go back after the surveyor says the same thing and try for a further reduction. You can, though, go back to the seller with the surveyor's report that the engine bearers are loose and agree a price reduction to allow you to have them refastened without having to foot the entire bill yourself.

In an extreme situation your having agreed to buy the boat 'subject to survey' will allow you to pull out of the deal, requesting the return of your deposit less any expenses involved in returning the boat to her original condition prior to the survey. That is to say, you must pay for the cost of slipping and relaunching (if required) together with any repainting or making good as a result of the surveyor having to remove linings or whatever in order to examine the boat thoroughly.

Broker's contract

If making use of the services of a reputable broker who is a member of either the Yacht Brokers, Designers and Surveyors Association (YBDSA) or the Association of Brokers and Yacht Agents (ABYA), he will adhere to the British Boating Industry Code of Practice for the Sale of Used Boats. This specifies such things as the holding of customers' deposits in separate clients' accounts and involves the broker in a fair amount of paperwork on your behalf. If you are buying a boat in an area remote from your home the broker will be able to provide you with the names and addresses of local surveyors, but he will be unable to

Plate 9.1. *The Maxi 84 is one of a range of boats bearing the Maxi name. Designed by Pelle Petterson and built in Sweden they offer good accommodation and sailing performance. Accommodation space is increased by carrying the cabin across the full width of the hull without any side decks. It makes for a big deck area too, which is easy to work on and pleasant for sunbathing in harbour. This boat is owned by a flotilla holiday company which, like any other kind of charter provides the potential boat buyer with a very good opportunity to try out the kind of boat he is thinking of buying before actually putting his money on the line.*

suggest any one in particular as that would be a breach of the Code of Practice.

Under that Code the broker will expect an initial deposit of 10% of the purchase price on acceptance by the vendor of your 'subject to survey' offer and will also expect the full transaction to be completed within 28 days.

The broker, incidentally, takes a commission on the agreed sale price from the vendor and nothing from you, the buyer, no matter how much work he does on your behalf.

Bills of Sale and receipts

In the case of registered boats it is essential to obtain a duly completed Bill of Sale when you buy so that you can re-register the boat in your name. Such a Bill will also be required by a finance company if you are seeking a marine mortgage or possibly any type of loan as it goes a long way towards proving title to the boat.

In the case of unregistered craft a Bill of Sale is a wise precaution, but even so it is essential to do your utmost to ensure that the boat is free from debt or you could end up with a writ on the mast for unpaid bills. Unless agreed otherwise the vendor should pay all outstanding yard and other bills to the date of completion of sale and that includes mortgage or loan payments, all of which must be discharged before the boat can be declared free of debt. The Bill of Sale describes this state as being 'free from encumbrance'.

One of the many jobs the broker undertakes is the discharge of any mortgage on the boat before he pays the balance of the sale price to the vendor, but if you are acting on your own behalf, then it is as well to obtain a written assurance that the mortgage has been or will be discharged within a given period.

When you are buying a boat and are going to take out a marine mortgage on her you will have to send the mortgage company your share of the purchase price (less the deposit already paid) and they will then make the full payment to the broker or vendor and undertake the transfer of title, re-registration and recording of the new mortgage on your behalf, which is a useful service as it saves you a lot of tedious paperwork.

You must of course, when making a private transaction, obtain written receipts for all moneys paid over to the vendor or his agent. In the case of the initial deposit, the receipt should state clearly that it is a refundable deposit subject to costs of restoration after the survey.

Deposits

The deposit on a secondhand boat is normally 10% of the agreed purchase price and it performs several functions. It shows the prospective purchaser's sincerity; it provides an actual sum of money from which the cost of returning the boat to her former condition can be paid in the event of a survey showing her to be unsatisfactory; it deters the buyer from backing out of the agreement despite a good survey report; and, if it is given to a broker, it is safeguarded for the purchaser in case the vendor suddenly decides to break his agreement, vanish or whatever.

The YBDSA provides its members with a highly suitable form of receipt and if you can obtain one of these for use in a private deal you would be well advised to do so.

Part ownership

The paperwork involved with buying a boat in partnership with one or more other people is no different from that when buying alone. Everything will have to have multiple signatures and establishing a loan may be either easier or harder depending on individual circumstances, but aside from that everything should go through just as smoothly.

The extra paperwork you might be well advised to undertake is a formal agreement between the partners made with the assistance of a solicitor. This document should pay particular attention to the details of what happens when one or more partners wants to sell their shares in the boat. It will also have to deal with the division of bills that have to be met and possibly the decision process behind any major expenditure. It might well be assumed that only like-minded and similarly financially placed people will form a partnership so that nobody will ask for anything outrageous to be bought and nobody will be in trouble tying to meet his share of the bills, but sadly life is not like that. Nor, as any divorce lawyer will tell you, do partners splitting up maintain their formerly cordial relations, therefore the exact process for anyone wanting to sell out or the decision to sell the boat entirely, must be carefully set down. It should actually make for a better partnership and may avoid the need for recourse to the legal document at all.

Time sharing

Time sharing of flats and holiday homes is quite popular, but time sharing of boats has not taken off on the same scale. By this system you buy a number of weeks' use of a boat each year for a set number of years. The boat is maintained for you (at your share of the cost) and is always ready for you to take away for your holiday period each year. It has its attractions, but there are several pitfalls, particularly on the maintenance side and there is always the possibility that mechanical breakdown or some other problem will mean that the boat is not available for you. The system also effectively ties you down to using the boat at the same time every year in the same area with little flexibility, even though some exchange systems are available.

If you do look at time sharing seriously, get a solicitor to go through the contract very carefully before you sign anything or part with any money. Obvious advice perhaps, but it could cost you a lot of money and heartache if you don't take it.

Registration

There are now two levels of registration in Britain. There is the full registration as a British ship and there is listing on the Small Ships Register. Full registration with the Registrar of British Ships will almost certainly be required if you are going to seek a marine mortgage to buy the boat and is required if you are to apply for an Admiralty warrant for the wearing of a blue ensign. Listing on the Small Ships Register, administered by the Royal Yachting Association, is much simpler and provides sufficient documentation when going abroad for example to France where registry papers are mandatory.

Full registration

Taking full registration first, the paperwork is fairly extensive, but much of it may be carried out on your behalf by the finance house giving you the mortgage or indeed by the broker. If the boat is already registered the problems are greatly reduced for it is then only necessary to have her re-registered in your name with the mortgage being recorded by the Registrar of British Ships at her port of registry. It costs of course, but does not take too long. If, on the other hand, you are buying an unregistered boat that has had several previous owners, it can be a very difficult job indeed to register her since each previous owner must be traced and various declarations obtained from them. With a very old boat this may actually prove impossible and you may therefore be unable to register her at all.

In the case of a new boat you will first have to apply to the Registrar of British Ships at your nearest port of registry (he is a Customs and Excise officer and usually to be found at the Custom House) to obtain the required forms. After that you need a builder's certificate declaring that the boat was built by his company and sold to you; a similar certificate from the engine manufacturer, though if the builder installed the engine he should give you this; the Registrar's approval of your chosen name for the boat, which must be unique amongst registered vessels; a certificate of measurement issued by a surveyor (preferably a YBDSA member); a declaration of ownership witnessed by a Commissioner for Oaths.

Once you have all those documents you send them to the Registrar who issues a Carving Note which gives you the boat's official number and name, both of which have to be inscribed in approved fashion in prescribed places on the boat and inspected by the surveyor who measured the boat (or another suitable one). Once that has been done and the appropriate fees paid the Registrar issues a Certificate of British Registry. The full process is set out in an RYA booklet or Notice No 382 available from Registrars.

Small Ships Register

This simpler scheme for those not wishing to obtain a marine mortgage but wanting to take their boats abroad, is administered by the Royal Yachting Association. The registration lasts for five years and is confined to privately, as opposed to company, owned boats of less than 24 metres in length, which are not fishing boats or 'submersible vessels'. Although there are exemptions in some European countries for very small boats, if you are considering taking *any* boat abroad it will make life easier if she is on the Small Ships Register.

For registration, a very simple form obtainable from the RYA is filled in and the only measurement required is the length overall, which can be measured by the owner. The form, together with the small registration fee, is then returned to the RYA who will issue you with an SSR registration number for display on the boat.

Boatyard and marina contracts

When you buy a boat you usually have to find a mooring as well and this will probably involve some sort of boatyard or marina berthing contract. In either case it is most important to read and understand the small print, which may include an abdication of responsibility for all or any accidents to you, your crew or your boat besides prohibiting the employment of any outside labour or contracted services and the levying of (usually) a 1% payment on the sale price of your boat if you decide to sell her from their premises. There may be much else besides and it really is important to know your liabilities and where you stand, so read it all.

Arranging deliveries

Whether you buy a new or secondhand boat you will have to move her to her new home port. In the case of dinghies and small boats, especially trailer sailers, it will probably be cheapest and best to undertake the delivery yourself, but in the case of larger craft you may wish to call on the services of a professional delivery company either for an overland or sea delivery.

Even quite large craft can be delivered by transporter overland, but for sea deliveries anything under about 25 ft will be impractical because of the likelihood of delay by bad weather. Such craft would be better loaded on a lorry and taken overland.

Boat transport and delivery companies advertise widely in the classified ads section of the yachting press and there is an association called the Yacht Delivery Association (see Appendix B) whose members use similar contracts and terms of business and can be relied upon to offer a good, safe, professional service. Considering the importance of protecting your new investment, it would be very unwise to employ just any unknown who sets himself up as a delivery skipper without any sort of credentials or indeed any of the many amateurs who offer to shift your boat because they want to make a trip from A to B. By shopping around a bit for best quotes you should find that (particularly on an overland delivery) you can save a lot if the delivery company can fit your boat in with a return trip. That is to say, if they can arrange to take a boat from A to B and then bring yours back from B to A (or nearby), both owners will have to foot smaller bills for fuel and time.

You must make sure that your boat is properly insured for the delivery, whether by sea or land, or request that the delivery company make the necessary arrangements at your expense. You must also ensure, particularly for a sea delivery, that the boat is in good order before the delivery crew goes aboard as it will save a lot of time, trouble and cost to you if they do not have to set to and make the boat seaworthy before beginning the delivery. Check through the contract to see what provisions are made for delays due to mechanical breakdown and stress of weather to see if there is any way you can minimize the cost. Finally, it is only human nature, that if a crew takes over a really clean, smart boat they will take that little bit extra care of her, so try to prepare the boat carefully before the delivery.

Part 2
Selling A Boat

10. Methods of Selling

Selling a boat can be a sad or a happy time depending on whether or not you really want to sell the boat and whether or not the sale is achieved easily on the terms you sought. Once you have made the decision to sell it is always best to get on with it as quickly as possible and that involves deciding how to sell: by private advertisement, through a broker or by part exchanging (trading in) the boat.

Private advertisements

Selling a boat through private advertisements may at first seem the cheapest way to go as there are no broker's fees to pay, but if you add up the costs of a series of advertisements and add on the time and trouble on your part in showing prospective purchasers over the boat, together, eventually, with handling all the paperwork involved in the sale, you may well discover that a broker is not as expensive as he first appears.

If you are going to advertise in a boating magazine it is first necessary to ensure that you put the ad in the most appropriate magazine for your type of boat. There are a large number of magazines on the bookstalls and most of them specialize in a particular sector of the boating field, so it is not difficult to find a good one for advertising any kind of boat from canal cruiser to skiboat or racing multihull. In fact it is likely that the right magazine will be the one you already read regularly.

Private ads for boats for sale are either small, brief classified paragraphs or semi-display ads with a longer blurb, a photo of the boat and an eyecatching presentation. It obviously costs more to insert a display ad than a simple classified and for, say, a class racing dinghy, it would be a waste of money putting in a series of display ads, but for a bigger boat, with a price tag of tens of thousands of pounds, the money could prove to be well spent. Unfortunately, you only know if it is worth it after the boat has been sold.

Whichever kind of advertisement you choose to use, it needs to be worded carefully in order to attract the potential buyer and to give him or her as much relevant information as possible without overwhelming him with detail. If you are selling a Bloggs 32 and therefore there will be several other Bloggs 32s being advertised in the same issue of the magazine you will have to rely on buyers being attracted either by the inclusion of a photograph, or by the price asked, or by the list of included equipment and/or location and age of the boat. On the other hand, if you are selling a well known, successful racing boat, you can make capital out of her name and her list of successes, making little mention of how she is equipped.

There is no magic formula for writing classified ads, but look at all the others for similar types of craft and see how they are worded, what is being offered and at what prices. You must not overprice your boat if you really want to sell her in a short period of time, spending as little on advertising as possible, but neither must you substantially underprice her as people will be made suspicious. Buyers usually have a good idea of general price levels and will wonder what is wrong with anything that is too low, even if it is accompanied by such words as 'for quick sale', 'owner has taken delivery of larger craft', 'marriage forces sale' or other such reasons.

The efficacy of including an explanation for the boat's sale in an ad is highly debatable. I would not do so as it can always be explained when contact is made with a potential buyer, but I would make sure that I know why I am selling as every buyer will ask. I also think it is best to be honest when giving a reply to such an enquiry, whether it is because you are buying another boat, can no longer afford to keep the boat or because your family is not interested in boating. If it is because there is something seriously wrong with the boat, it is up to you and your conscience whether or not you admit to it, but remember that a good surveyor will find most troubles out.

If you are not going to overwhelm the reader of the advertisement with a long and detailed list of included equipment it is as well to write or type one out and have a few photocopies run off together with full details of the boat so that you can mail them out to interested enquirers. In the ad you only have to say that there is a good or full inventory including electronics or whatever and say 'details available from' then give your phone number, address or a box number at the magazine.

Speaking personally, I like to phone for details of a boat as it is faster than writing and I always wonder why a box number is used, but then perhaps I am just suspicious by nature. If you do give a phone number, say 'after 6 pm' if that is when you will be there (or whenever) and try to be available in the first few days after the ad appears. There is nothing more annoying than to ring about a boat and be asked to ring again later. It is better if necessary for whoever takes the call to ask for a number on which you can ring back. In any case, keep a copy of the boat details handy to the phone so that you have the answers to hand as it always sounds better to the buyer if you appear to know the important facts about the boat you are selling.

How many times you decide initially to insert the advertisement is up to you, but it is probably worth putting it in at least twice to begin with. That way you should catch the occasional readers as well as the regulars.

Brokers

Yacht brokers take a commission on the achieved sale price of any boat they sell and consequently appear expensive, but in fact they do a lot of work and a good one will spend quite a bit on advertising the boats they have for sale, both by way of advertisements in magazines and by direct mailing shots to interested buyers whose names they have on file.

The commission rate is currently 8% on boats in the UK and 10% on boats lying abroad. Charges are of course subject to VAT at the current rate, but include the 1% (or whatever) that the boatyard or marina takes on the sale of your boat from their premises under the terms of your berthing contract with them. This charge would be payable from your selling price even in the event of a private sale.

Although it may seem an easy way of earning a living, a good broker who is a member of either the Yacht Brokers Designers and Surveyors Association or the Association of Brokers and Yacht Agents, actually works very hard for his commission on the majority of sales. There will always be the occasional plum that falls neatly into his lap, but usually he will have to prepare a detail sheet on the boat including a colour photo, mail it to likely buyers registered with him, advertise in magazines, answer calls about the boat, show people over her, act as go-between during the purchase negotiations, give advice to both sides and finally undertake all the complicated paperwork of Bills of Sale, registration and so on, even perhaps helping the buyer to arrange finance. He takes many of the headaches out of selling a boat and for that alone deserves adequate reward, but it is important to place your boat on the books of a good broker. If you keep a good dog, you don't have to bark yourself.

Members of the YBDSA or ABYA adhere to a code of professional conduct and carry professional indemnity insurance, so you can, if all else fails and everything goes wrong, sue them. Everyone hopes it won't come to that, but it is a reassuring safeguard.

Because a broker is dealing with the selling of boats all the time, he is a very good source of advice on the whole process from setting the right price to how to present the boat to a potential buyer. Talk to him and listen to his advice, particularly regarding price. You can set whatever price you like and it is unlikely that he will actually refuse to advertise the boat at that price, but if he suggests it is over the top and you are anxious to sell the boat, you would do well to think again as he knows the market and what the boat is eventually going to fetch.

You will have to provide the broker with a detailed specification for the boat and it is sensible to show him over her personally as you will be able to answer his queries on the spot.

Computer listings

One or two firms operate computer listings of boats for sale both privately and through brokers. These computer agencies do not act in the same way as brokers, who take a commission on the selling price, but more like classified ads, in that they accept a single flat rate fee from the boat owner and simply distribute the details of the boat to those requesting them. They have no part in the transaction nor do they require any further payment.

Prospective boat buyers contact the computer agency, specifying their requirements and the agency sends them details of suitable boats on their data files together with the names and addresses of their owners. The potential buyer then selects the ones that interest him and contacts the owners. Thereafter you treat the sale as a private one with the computer firm taking no further part.

By placing your boat on the data files of a computer agency you know exactly what your 'advertising' costs are going to be and you can reach people in quite unexpected places. Instead of placing a classified advertisement in one or two specialist magazines you allow yourself the chance of reaching people who never look at those magazines but who are, nonetheless, anxious to buy a boat like yours.

You must, as with any form of private advertisement, have a prepared description and detail sheet for your boat and also be ready to show prospective buyers over the boat. You will also have to negotiate with them face to face rather than through the third party of a broker and to carry out all the necessary paperwork yourself. All of this means putting yourself to some inconvenience and investing some time and energy, but it saves on broker's fees.

Boatyards and marinas

Most boatyards and marinas run some form of brokerage section, whether it is a very minor operation or a full scale business with a separate on-site office. They will charge the same rates as any other broker, but may have a slight advantage in being able to help a prospective buyer to find a berth for the boat. Aside from that though they have little to offer that other brokers do not. Their commission should take care of the one per cent charged by many yards and marinas on sales negotiated on their premises.

The drawback to a small boatyard brokerage operation is that they are more than likely to do little other than hand out information to those that come knocking on their doors. Many of them do little in the way of advertising or maintaining mailing lists. It is usually the bigger businesses that do this.

However, they are on the spot for showing people over your boat and they should know her quite well. Also, they are likely to hear of any local people that are interested in your type of craft.

Noticeboards

Most clubhouses, chandlers, waterside post offices and newsagents all maintain noticeboards on which, for a small sum, you can display a postcard advertising your boat for sale. The effectiveness of these advertisements varies enormously, but their cost is so low that it is well worth backing up any other form of advertising with a notice on every board you can find.

Word of mouth

This too can be a surprisingly effective way of selling your boat and is certainly cheap! Just let it be known in a few ears that you are looking to sell your boat and the news will get around. If she is that kind of boat, you will find that the information reaches the right people within the locality and that may be all that is needed. Like noticeboard ads, word of mouth cannot be relied on but is a useful supplement.

Non-boating press

Of the non-boating press *Exchange & Mart* is the favourite place to advertise boats for sale of all types. The readership is enormous and many boat owners buy the paper when they are looking for items of gear or equipment and even if they are not actively trying to buy a boat, the casual reader may have his imagination fired by the right kind of classified ad. It is probably well worth a try for a few weeks.

Local newspapers too may be worth advertising in, as they are commonly taken by local residents and even weekend visitors. National newspapers are rather too expensive to advertise anything but the most expensive types of boat in and can effectively be ignored.

Auctions

Boat auctions tend to be last resorts for desperate boat owners. This is probably not strictly true, but it is a widespread impression as the buyer can do no more than make a superficial examination of the boats and bid for them 'as seen'. When you are trying to sell a boat, I guess it is up to you. You can put a reserve price on the boat but beyond that you have no control over the selling price and you will have to pay the auctioneer's fees. Also, you will have to get the boat to the auction (and home again if she is not sold).

Secondhand boat shows

There are now several secondhand boat shows during the course of the year and if there is one at your home port (or nearby), it would be worth considering putting your boat on display. You would have to investigate the commission charged together with the costs of slipping or berthing for the duration of the show, but they are popular events with buyers who have the chance to see several boats at the same time.

When the secondhand show is run in conjunction with a new boat show you may catch the buyer who decides he wants a particular class of boat but cannot stretch to a new version. If yours is a good example of the class, but a couple of years old, you may just find yourself a good buyer, quickly.

11. Preparing a Boat for Sale

First impressions carry a lot of weight with boat buyers and there is a far greater chance of making a sale if the boat gives an immediate impression of being in good, cared for condition. A boat lying awkwardly in a mud berth with a bent stanchion poking through a chafed hole in the winter cover does not appeal to the potential buyer, while the same boat, snuggling against a marina pontoon with a clean, carefully secured cover and an air of dormant readiness for sea is already half sold.

Far too many owners reach a decision in the latter part of the season to sell at the end of it and immediately lose all further interest in their craft. They virtually abandon the boat as soon as the ads are inserted or the broker instructed and then sit back and wonder why nobody wants to buy her.

If you want the top price for your boat (meaning the top realistic price) you must be prepared to put some effort into getting her ready for inspection by people who probably have a wide range of boats to choose from and are not about to throw their hard won money away on one that will need weeks of work to bring her up to scratch. Buyers expect to have to do some fitting out work before beginning the season, but with so many secondhand boats on the market they can be very choosy about what they buy.

Paint and varnish

A lick of paint and a coat of varnish can do wonders for a boat's appearance, but it is equally well known that they can hide a multitude of problems. Trying to hide, for example, a patch of rot by painting over it is a waste of time as any surveyor worth his salt will find the rot anyway. If you decide for some reason to sell your boat immediately after spring fitting out, it is reasonable that she should be freshly painted and varnished without a mark on her, but at any other time of the year it is sensible to repair damaged paint and brightwork without going to the expense of a full coating. You probably won't recoup the cost of the paint or of your time and may make a potential buyer suspicious, whereas if you have clearly made an effort to tidy the boat up and prevent further damage by ingress of water, you demonstrate your continuing care for the boat and openness in not trying to hide anything. If you decide to sell at the end of the season, do not skimp on your normal winter lay-up routine, because your protective efforts will pay off if you don't succeed in selling before the next season.

GRP topsides

The topsides of a glassfibre boat tend to show all the scuffs and marks of a season's use quite clearly, but can be cleaned and polished to restore a fine, attractive shine quite easily. Deeper gouges and chips should be filled, sanded and polished to prevent further deterioration just as they would be at the end of any normal season. Doing this will make the boat look better to anyone inspecting her and will save time and trouble later if you fail to sell as planned.

As with repainting a wooden boat, it is probably not worth having a glassfibre one resprayed before selling unless the gelcoat is really badly faded or scarred as the cost of the job will be hard to recover in the selling price. However, if there are any signs of osmosis in the gelcoat of the bottom or around the waterline you will almost certainly have to have repairs done. Osmosis can be cured in almost all cases, but is a total sale killer and although the cost of major repairs may be high, you will have no choice but to have them done.

Sails, spars and rigging

Here again it is worth taking a little trouble to bring things up to standard. Sails can be valetted by sailmakers or repairers at reasonable cost and will come out much better on a surveyor's report if they are clean and free from chafed stitching, torn panels and loose hanks or slides. The fact that a sail is patched may not attract a buyer, but if it has been professionally done it should not put him off, even if he is expecting to race the boat, for such a buyer will (or should) realize that a new sail is going to be a natural hazard to his wallet.

If sails are sent for valetting they should be back and available for inspection by the time interested buyers are shown over the boat and those that do not require such attention should be carefully folded or rolled and bagged up rather than just pushed into a sailbag all higgledy-piggledy. Modern materials such as Mylar just can't cope with such handling and it demonstrates a lack of care that may be extended to other parts of the boat.

Spars that are dented or damaged in any way will naturally be viewed with suspicion and it is therefore worth getting the spar maker to check them over and if he considers them to be still sound, see if you can get a written report out of him to show a surveyor.

Standing rigging must of course be in good condition without kinks, broken strands or bent bottlescrews or terminals. Any such problems will mean replacement either at your direct expense or in a negotiated drop in the asking price – even though you may argue that you have taken them into account when setting the asking price. Running rigging too needs to be in reasonable condition. Any used sheet or rope halyard will show a bit of chafe and with core and sheath construction ropes this is actually not a bad thing as they will then hold better on winch barrels, but it should not be excessive. Where there are cuts or excessive chafe you must again consider renewal or an allowance in the selling price.

Engines

It is definitely worth spending some time cleaning up the engine. It does not need to sparkle with burnished copper fuel pipes and a chromed rocker box cover, but larger areas of gunge and accumulated oil should be cleaned off. The engine needs to look used, but well maintained without giving too many hints that you have tarted it up just for the buyer's inspection. Just make it look as though it has not been totally ignored so long as it ran. Make sure there is actually some oil in the sump and gearbox and that the stern gland greaser contains enough grease.

Motor boat owners might consider providing details of

maintenance intervals with notes such as the need to change oil filters in another 20 hours (or whatever). Certainly some knowledge of running hours since the last service and of such things as operating revs will be essential, either to tell a buyer directly or through the broker. It is like all the rest of the boat; do not overdo things, but an obvious care and interest in the engine(s) will influence a potential buyer in your boat's favour.

Accommodation

The accommodation area of a laid up boat can all too easily become damp and smelly, so do ensure that the boat is adequately ventilated, including locker spaces. Thoroughly clean the heads compartment so that it is both clean and fresh as there is nothing more off-putting to anyone looking over a boat than to find a smelly, dirty loo compartment.

The galley area must be cleared of all foodstuffs, both perishable and canned, leaving only what is to be sold with the boat. Clean thoroughly to remove all traces of grease and dead food. This, like the heads, is an area that repays all the work you put into it and there is no limit to how clean and sparkly you should make it – and that includes crockery, cutlery, pots and pans if these are to be sold with the boat.

As for the rest of the accommodation, it will depend on circumstances whether you leave berth cushions on board or not, but if you do, beware of mildew. Thoroughly clean and air the entire accommodation and try to make it look inviting. Older wooden boats when laid up for the winter are normally left with lockers open and cabin sole boards lifted, but this makes it difficult to move about down below and on a modern glassfibre boat is probably better to leave things in place but ensure good ventilation as far as possible.

A clean, tidy interior complete with berth cushions and so on is undoubtedly more attractive than a bare cabin, but the latter may be more practical and should not be considered too detrimental as it may actually avoid problems in the form of mildew and musty smells.

Gear and equipment

Everything not for sale should be removed from the boat. Everything for sale should either be on board or readily available for inspection. Everything listed in the inventory must be available and must work unless listed as being defective; this is a legal requirement.

Aside from those comments it should be fairly apparent that a poor impression will be created if too much gear and equipment is either missing as it is being repaired or missing because it is not for sale. Just how much equipment you include is up to you, but a fully equipped boat will sell faster than one that is pretty bare, even though the sale prices achieved may not be sufficiently different to cover the cost of the equipment included. You have to weigh up the importance of a quick sale against being able to carry equipment over to your own next boat (assuming that she will not have that equipment already installed).

You may decide to remove (say) a radar set, but state that it is available at a certain additional price. I cannot say whether this is good salesmanship or not, it is for you to decide having regard to the actual item of equipment and the general circumstances, but whatever you decide, it must be clear what is included and what is not included in the asking price.

Repairing damage

It seems a fair assertion that a 'whole' boat is far more saleable than a badly damaged one, even though the latter may carry a much lower price tag. Few people actually want to carry out major repair work before they can use their new purchase. They may be prepared for a bit of work – say a new rudder – but they don't want to have to wait for a yard to carry out major structural repairs and then foot the bill at the end of it, however low the purchase price was.

Just what level of damage you can leave is hard to say. Things like bent stanchions should be replaced as they smack of neglect, as would a broken propeller blade. On the other hand you may prefer not to replace a split hatch cover, but in the end I think it comes down to how badly you want to sell the boat. If a repair will not cost a lot it is better to have it done rather than let a potential buyer be put off through wondering what other damage was caused at the same time.

If you do not want to go to the trouble of having major work done – for example a hole in the hull repaired – you will have to admit to the damage from the outset. Do not drag someone half way across the country to view the boat and then tell him what major work needs doing.

12. Practical Selling

As I have the general impression that I couldn't sell straws to a drowning man, I feel poorly qualified to write about salesmanship to an audience possibly including professional salesmen, but there are various points that need bringing out. To begin with, before worrying about where to advertise and what to say in the ad, give careful consideration to what happens when someone wants to view your boat.

Locating the boat

It will make a poor impression on the visitor if they have to tramp across miles of mud to reach a secluded mud berth or wait shivering on the bank for the tide to rise enough for a wet row out to the moored craft. They may be put off too by a complicated set of directions for finding an off the map boatyard.

There are centres for boating dotted all round our coastline where boats of a type are concentrated together. You may not normally wish to, be able to afford to, or be able to find a mooring on which to keep your boat in these popular areas, but for the purposes of selling her it may be a distinct advantage to locate a temporary berth at a popular spot, preferably a walk-aboard marina. If you do so, visitors will be able to reach the place easily and get aboard your boat without any fuss, which will mean they start looking at the boat in an unruffled, receptive frame of mind.

Having the boat in a marina usually means that you can get in

Plate 12.1. *A clear demonstration of the difference in draught between a bilge keeler (dark hull) and a lifting keel boat (white hull). The latter is all but afloat in ankle deep water, while the bilge keeler must wait quite a time yet for the rising tide to lift her off.*

and out at pretty well any time, making demonstration sails easier. You do not have to tell your prospective buyers to arrive at awkward times if they want to sail and then have to keep them out for 12 hours waiting for the next tide.

Moving the boat to a temporary berth may be expensive and make travelling more difficult for you, but if it means an easier sale it will be worthwhile and if it puts the boat within easier reach of a good broker you may be saved the trouble of journeying to and fro yourself, leaving the inspections to him.

A move to a more favourable location may help in the sale of any boat, but if yours is an out-of-production production boat or a strange one-off, it will be particularly important as you will already have a difficult task on your hands. There is no real reason why a boat no longer built should be harder to sell than one still in production, or why a good one-off should put buyers off, but the fact is that, statistically, both of these types are harder to sell. That means getting everything possible on your side and to that end listening to the advice of a good, possibly a specialist, broker will be to your advantage.

Showing customers over

When someone asks to see your boat you must do your utmost to make yourself available at the time or on the day that suits the customer, again making things easy for him. Arrange a date and time and make sure you are early. That gives you a chance, particularly if you have not been aboard for some time, to open the boat up, get a bit of air through, and make sure everything is all right. Check through as much of the boat as you can to see that there is no dripping condensation, mildew, full bilges, corroded electrics or a seized up engine. *Remember that anything listed on the 'for sale' inventory must be in working order unless you have stated that it is defective*, so it is as well before the customer arrives to run over everything quickly, replacing batteries where necessary and so on. That way you do not have to worry if, for example, the echo sounder or wind instruments are switched on during the visit.

Even if the boat is laid up ashore you should give yourself a bit of time beforehand to air the boat and generally check her over. A laid up boat always has a dormant atmosphere about her, but she should still be clean and tidy. Close locker doors, re-lay sole boards, put the engine casing back and generally try to make it easier for the unfamiliar visitor to move about and feel welcome. Also, if the boat is laid up ashore, try to provide a secure ladder or set of steps for boarding.

When the visitors do arrive, try to give them a friendly reception without overwhelming them and giving them the idea that they are seen as the answer to a desperate prayer.

You will have to provide some sort of guided tour of the boat, but avoid being too effusive in your praise of her. Talk positively about good features, demonstrating briefly whatever needs explanation, answer questions at any stage and once you have gone through the boat, offer to leave the visitors alone for a few minutes to take a look by themselves. If they accept this offer, depart and occupy yourself somehow while remaining alert to their readiness for you to return. That is probably the time to offer to show them any sails or equipment not on the boat.

Similarly, with a boat that is still in commission, give the potential customer a chance to look carefully over the boat before suggesting that you leave on your planned demonstration sail.

During your guided tour remember to offer relevant information, such as the number of hours the engines have been run since the last major overhaul, how much fuel they consume or do a little bragging (not too much) about your racing successes during the season. Just push a little, but don't overdo it.

You will have to judge the situation for yourself, but if the visitors seem interested and you think the time is right, then do offer them a cup of tea or coffee if the galley is operative or you have thought to bring a flask and mugs with you. It is often over a warming cuppa that a deal can be clinched. However, if you are actually selling through a broker, even though you are showing people over the boat yourself, it may be wiser to let the buyer make his formal offer through the broker. You can quite well reach an agreement between yourselves on the basis that you would accept a figure if it were offered and he can then go off and telephone the broker to make that offer, but it is better to have it all set up properly through the broker as he can then deal with the deposit and all the rest of the paperwork and earn his commission. It also keeps a buffer between you and the buyer in case anything goes wrong with the deal.

In the case of a private sale you will obviously have to be prepared to do your bargaining face to face or later by phone, but in either case you should have decided already what price you will accept and be resolute in your determination to hold out for it. Don't bother to try the old 'I have somebody else who's very interested' ploy unless you genuinely have, in which case it is only fair to warn another interested party if someone else has a prior option. Also, unless the offer made is patently ridiculous, don't snort and tell the man he must be joking when he makes his offer. That way you will certainly lose the sale. Rather state simply that you cannot drop the price that far but are open to a more reasonable offer.

You should also be prepared, once you accept an offer (probably subject to survey) to deal with a 10 per cent deposit. It is as well to provide a written receipt stating the agreed sale price, the amount of the deposit, that it is returnable, the fact that it is an offer subject to survey and if you can, obtain the offer in writing again stating that it is subject to survey, but also stating that the sale will be completed within an agreed period, normally 28 days, in order to avoid procrastination and delays on either side. It is in areas like this that the broker is so useful.

When you accept the cheque for the deposit it is as well to get your bank to do an express clearance. They will charge you grossly for this service, but that way you find out quickly if all is well and will have an easier mind when you have to tell other people who contact you that a sale has been agreed on the boat.

Demonstration sails

Taking people out for a demonstration sail should not be too much of a problem in fair weather, but you have to be prepared to call it off if the weather is too bad. If that is the case, try to co-operate in the arranging of another date and hope for better luck then.

So far as you are concerned, as vendor of the boat, a demonstration sail should be just that, an opportunity to show how well the boat sails, how easily and how steadily, or how nicely she handles in and out of locks or how smoothly and swiftly she pulls a water skier or whatever her forte is supposed to be. You as owner should be familiar with all her handling characteristics and should be able to show them off to best advantage. I don't mean by making a series of flash manoeuvres that might go badly wrong, but by working the boat with obvious ease and pleasure.

Draw attention to good features of the boat or her performance and if you can, put her through her paces before allowing the prospective buyer to have his turn. You can't hog the helm, but from your point of view this is your chance to give a demonstration of the boat's capabilities before the buyer tries to find out if the boat will suit him and possibly misses an important good point.

You will always make a good impression on a potential buyer if you appear genuinely fond of the boat and sorry to be parting with her even if you are excited about your next purchase. Don't keep saying how fond you are of her, but let it be clearly understood.

Launching and slipping

If a buyer wants to have a boat slipped for survey or launched for trials, the cost, together with the cost of restoring the boat to her previous condition, is his responsibility, if necessary deductible from his 10% deposit. This is certainly the principle, but it does not always work out exactly that way in practice. A friend of mine once epoxy painted the bottom of his glassfibre cruiser, antifouled her and a few days later she was surveyed. The surveyor, wondering what was under the epoxy paint, scraped off numerous patches, thus destroying its effectiveness as a barrier and all my friend was able to obtain in recompense was the cost of dabbing some antifouling over the bare patches, without any epoxy underneath.

It is hard to say that this sort of situation should not be allowed to arise, but it shouldn't. A buyer should therefore be reminded of his responsibilities before he commissions a survey and he should then instruct the surveyor to do as little damage as possible. Again a broker may be in a stronger position to accomplish compensation than a private seller.

The launching and slipping costs can be more easily recovered from the buyer as he will have to make suitable arrangements with the boatyard or marina and they can bill him directly. Just remember to point all this out to the buyer when you accept his offer and if you can, get it down in writing. Solicitors always like that, but let's hope it never gets that far.

13. The Paperwork of Selling

Offers subject to survey

Normally you will be made an offer for your boat taking into account faults that the buyer has found during his initial inspection of her and that offer will be made 'subject to survey'. Assuming you accept either that first offer or can haggle with the prospective buyer until you reach a mutually acceptable figure, you will be agreeing to sell your boat for the agreed price on condition that a surveyor commissioned by the buyer does not reveal any serious defects and is able to give the boat a reasonably clean bill of health.

Should the surveyor turn up some major or at least expensive fault, the buyer may come back to you with a revised (lower) offer and you must then decide whether or not to accept it or try to negotiate a new agreed figure. Remember when trying to do this that any other potential buyer's surveyor is almost certainly going to find the same defect, so you are unlikely to be able to avoid making a monetary allowance for it at some time in the selling process.

All survey reports make a boat look as though she is a near total wreck or at least in need of substantial repairs, so if a buyer does come back with a reduced offer, ask to see a copy of the report, or at least the relevant section, and if necessary consult a builder regarding repair costs. That way you will have a good idea of what a reasonable settlement figure would be when the buyer makes his new offer.

It must be remembered that if a survey report is not satisfactory and you cannot reach agreement with the prospective buyer, he is entitled to withdraw his offer on the boat and receive a refund of his deposit less costs of restoring the boat after her survey.

The making of an offer 'subject to survey' is obviously of advantage to the buyer rather than the vendor, but you would be daft not to agree to the condition else you are unlikely to sell your boat at all.

Broker's contract

When you are selling your boat through a broker he will act as go-between, relaying offers and counter-offers between vendor and purchaser. Once the sale has been agreed he will take a 10% deposit from the purchaser and immediately change his role from that of vendor's agent to 'stakeholder' or neutral party, and he will be described as such in any written matter. This is all laid out in the standard form of contract used by members of the Yacht Brokers, Designers and Surveyors Association and the Association of Brokers and Yacht Agents. The agreement, which is a model for any private transactions as well, covers all eventualities with regard to the results of the survey being unsatisfactory, the deposits, Bills of Sale, completion of payment, insurance and so on. By using one of these agreements both parties to the transaction know exactly where they stand and it is an agreement well worth copying if you make a private purchase. Indeed the agreement is one very strong reason for employing a good broker when selling as he will look after your interests and protect you from any wrangling or problems.

Finally, don't forget that it is you, the vendor, who is paying the broker, so his commission comes out of your agreed sale price, but if there is a percentage due to the boatyard or marina where your boat is kept, that should come out of the broker's commission.

Bills of Sale

Provision of a Bill of Sale is essential in the case of a registered boat but is advisable on all craft. From the buyer's point of view it effectively transfers title in the boat to him and prevents the vendor trying to come back for more money later, while from the vendor's side it relieves him of any liability for bills incurred after the date of the sale.

When selling your boat you will be liable for all outstanding debts including yard bills for moorings or storage, sailmaker's and chandler's bills, mortgages or other loans and so on, up to the date of completion of the sale. In some cases the broker will settle these bills from the money paid over to him by the purchaser or his mortgage or loan company before paying the balance of the sale price over to you. The freedom of the boat from any debts is stated on the Bill of Sale where she is described as 'free from encumbrance'.

Bills of Sale for private vendors can be obtained from HM Customs and Excise offices.

Deposits and receipts

When you agree a sale price for your boat you can expect to receive a 10% deposit either directly in the case of a private sale or to the broker (acting as stakeholder) in the case of a sale through a broker. This deposit performs several functions: it demonstrates your intention to sell and the purchaser's intention to buy; it provides an actual sum of money from which the costs of returning the boat to her former condition can be paid in the event of a survey showing her to be unsatisfactory; it deters the buyer from backing out of the agreement despite a good survey report; and if given to a broker (stakeholder) it is safeguarded for the purchaser in case the vendor suddenly decides to break the agreement and not sell the boat.

Naturally, when handing over an often substantial sum of money, the purchaser will require a written receipt. In the case of a broker belonging to either the Yacht Brokers, Designers and Surveyors Association or the Association of Brokers and Yacht Agents, they will use a proper form supplied by those associations, but in the case of a private sale you will have to draw up a receipt unless you can get a form from one of the associations. If you provide the receipt yourself it must accept the money as a deposit against the full (stated) sale price; it must say that it is a refundable deposit subject to the outcome of the survey if one is to be commissioned; it should state a date for completion of the sale (usually 28 days later); it should state that deductions from the deposit can be made for costs involved in returning the boat to her former condition after the survey in the event of the sale falling through. An attachment listing the included inventory may be requested by the buyer and should be provided.

It would also be as well from the vendor's point of view to obtain an equivalent written statement from the purchaser stating his intention to purchase subject to survey with completion within 28 days of agreement.

Receiving the money

The most direct method of payment is clearly a bundle of pound notes, but other than on the sale of very small craft you are more likely to have to accept either a personal cheque, a cheque from a building society or loan company or a bank draft. In the case of a personal cheque, which can be stopped by the purchaser, it is obviously in your interest to get it paid into your account as quickly as possible. To achieve that it may be necessary to pay your bank an (exorbitant) amount for an 'express' clearance and notification of the fact that it has been cleared.

It is wise if at all possible, to allow the purchaser to take actual possession of the boat only after his cheque for the balance of the purchase price has been cleared. This will all be dealt with for you by a broker if you are selling through one, but if you make a private sale you may have to say face to face that you must get the cheque cleared before handing the boat over.

Cheques from building societies, loan companies or banks can be trusted as they will not be stopped once issued, but make sure they are made out correctly in terms of the sum and particularly your name together with the right date.

Inventory

When agreeing to sell your boat you should provide the purchaser with a list of the gear and equipment that is included. This inventory will already have been requested by a broker, but in a private sale it is as well to supply it at this stage and in any written agreement between yourself and the purchaser it should be referred to. This can be done so that you agree to sell/purchase the boat (named) at a price (stated) to include the inventory as per attached schedule (and attach a copy of the list).

The inventory should include all items in detail and remember that unless listed as being defective, each item of equipment must be in working order. You will find that on any boat the list is quite extensive as it should include engines, paddles, sails, spars, crockery, the lot.

Insurance

Once the sale has been completed and you have received all due money, it is time to contact your insurers and inform them that you have sold the boat. You may then either be eligible for a refund on your premium or it may be held in abeyance against your purchasing another boat in the near future. In either case wait until you are sure you no longer require the cover and then inform the company quickly so as to gain maximum rebate or carry-over.

Appendix A: Some Common Terms and Abbreviations Used in Classified Boat Advertisements

Afrormosia: A durable hardwood. Difficult to work as it is cross-grained.

Any survey: Owner confident boat is in sound condition and would pass any survey. It's no guarantee though and you will still have to have the boat surveyed.

Aries: Type of wind vane self-steering gear.

Autohelm: Electronic autopilot.

Aux: Auxiliary engine. Not commonly used in ads today as few boats do not have an engine.

Avon: Very popular make of inflatable dinghy.

B & G Brookes & Gatehouse, make of electronic instruments.

Bm: Bermudan rigged (often assumed these days).

BS1088: British Standards Institution's minimum construction requirements for marine plywood.

Bailer: Self-bailer fitted in bottom of racing dinghies.

Bilge keels: Twin ballasted keels allowing boat to have shallow draught and sit upright when aground.

Blake: Baby Blake. Make of marine toilet.

c/b: Centreboard (wood).

CRE: Canadian Rock Elm. A timber used for planking hulls.

c/w: Complete with.

Canoe stern: Stern pointed like bow.

Carvel: Wooden hull with planks fitted edge to edge and the gaps between 'caulked' to close them.

Cascover: Trade name of a fabric matrix for epoxy sheathing wood, either hull or decks.

Cathedral: Hull shape of small powerboat which looks as though it has three hulls like a squashed trimaran.

Certificate: Certificate of measurement for class racing dinghy, essential if racing intended.

Chute: Tube into which spinnaker is recovered and from which it is set.

Clinker: Wooden hull with each plank overlapping the next one below.

Cold moulded: Hull construction employing glued layers of wood veneers resulting in a light, strong hull. Usually only used for one-off hulls.

Combi trolley: A combined launching trolley and road trailer.

Combo bag: A bag designed to carry the daggerboard, tiller, cordage, blocks and battens for a Laser dinghy.

Composite hull: Either combination of glassfibre hull and wooden decks or a hi-tech sandwich of resin and a core matrix.

Current IOR: Has valid offshore racing certificates.

DF: Radio Direction Finder.

DWL: Designed waterline length which may differ from actual waterline length (LWL).

Deep V: Underwater hull shape of powerboat which looks like a V when viewed from head on.

Dinette: An arrangement of seats and table in main cabin which converts to a double berth.

Dory: A flat, open, outboard powered runabout.

Double diagonal: Construction method for hull, employing two layers of wood laid diagonally over moulds with outer layer at an angle to inner skin. Generally only found in older craft.

Double ender: Boat with canoe stern.

Drop keel: Like centreplate, but major part of ballast concentrated in the lifting keel.

EC: As in 'lying EC', east coast.

E/S: Echo sounder.

Electrics: As in 'full electrics', usually meaning batteries, internal and navigation lights plus electric starting and charging on the engine.

Electronics: Instruments such as log, echo sounder, RDF etc.

Ferro: Ferrocement. Hull constructed of reinforced concrete.

Fin: Keel form which is narrow and deep. Well separated from rudder.

Flush deck: Very little in the way of cabin or other superstructure above the decks. Makes working on deck easier.

Flying bridge: A remote steering and control position, usually atop the wheelhouse but sometimes on a tower structure, for motor boats.

Foam sandwich: Construction method using a layer of closed cell foam between skins of glassfibre.

Fractional rig: Forestay terminating some distance below masthead.

GRP: Glassfibre, though it actually stands for glass reinforced polyester.

Gunning: Type of wind vane self steering gear.

H & C: Hot and cold pressurized water system.

Hasler: Type of wind vane self steering gear.

Headfoil: A grooved plastic or alloy (aluminium) cover or replacement for the forestay that takes the luff of the headsail instead of its being hanked on to a wire stay.

IOR IIIa: International Offshore Rule Mark IIIa. A measurement and handicapping system for offshore racing boats.

Inboard/outboard: An inboard engine installed to drive a steerable external drive leg and propeller. Same as outdrive.

Inflatable: A pump-up dinghy which can be deflated then stowed more easily while on passage than a rigid dinghy.

Iroko: An African hardwood of great durability.

Jammers: Jamming cleats.

Kevlar: Trade name for carbon fibre based material used for reinforcing hulls and in construction of rope.

LOA: Length overall, roughly from stem to stern *excluding* bowsprit or bumkin.

l/s: Longshaft (outboard engine).

l/trolley: Launching trolley.

LWL: Load waterline length. Length on the waterline when boat is fully equipped.

Lavac: Popular type of sea toilet evacuated by vacuum pump.

Legs: Detachable supports allowing a single keeled boat to dry out standing upright.

Lifting keel: Like centreplate, but major portion of ballast concentrated in the lifting plate. Same as drop keel.

Log: Distance recorder.

Long keel: Ballast keel running much of length of boat with rudder hung on after end.

MFV: Motor fishing vessel (usually converted from).

m/h rig: Masthead rig. Forestay terminates at masthead.

MTB: Motor torpedo boat (usually converted from).

MV: Motor vessel.

MY: Motor yacht.

Mahogany on oak: Boat constructed of mahogany planks fastened over oak frames.

Main: Mainsail.

Marine ply: Plywood made with special glues to resist delamination in marine environment. Should conform to BS1088 and carry BSI kite mark.

Marine toilet: A toilet that evacuates directly overboard.

Mylar: Modern material used in sailcloth especially for racing boats; does not like rough usage.

Navik: Type of wind vane self steering.

Neco: Type of autopilot.

o/b: Outboard engine.

ono: Or nearest offer. Owner is open to negotiation on asking price.

One-off: Single boat to individual design as opposed to series production boat.

Outdrive: Same as inboard/outboard. Inboard engine connected to steerable, outboard drive leg.

Pilot: Any autopilot.

Pine: Often used as abbreviation for pitch pine, but beware as they are quite different. Pine is a softwood of low durability.

Pinta: Type of autopilot.

Pitch pine: Resinous wood of fair durability.

Porta-Potti: Self-contained but flushing chemical toilet.

Pram: Transom (blunt) bowed dinghy used as tender.

Pramhood: Foldaway fabric shelter over companionway.

Pulpit, pushpit: Rails round bow and stern respectively, connected on each side of boat by guardrails which are in turn supported by stanchions.

RDF: Radio direction finder.

RT: Radio telephone.

Regd: Registered as a British Ship (full registration).

r/reefing: Roller reefing.

s/bailer: Self bailer.

s/d: Self draining (cockpit).

slp: Sloop rigged.

SL400: Type of marine toilet made by Simpson Lawrence.

SS, s/s: Stainless steel or self-steering depending on context.

SSB: Single side band radio telephone.

SSDY: Single screw diesel yacht.

SSR: Small ships register. RYA organized registration system for foreign cruising without complexity and cost of full registration.

Saildrive, S-drive: Type of drive unit made by Volvo Penta for use on fin keeled yachts. Engine close coupled through bottom of hull to drive leg like that of an outdrive, but which is not steerable.

Sandwich: Construction method employing a core matrix sandwiched between layers of glassfibre.

Seafarer: Make of echo sounder.

Seagull: Make of outboard engine.

Sea toilet: One that evacuates directly overboard.

Semi-balanced rudder: Part of the blade area is ahead of the pivot (stock) to make steering lighter.

Skeg rudder: Rudder hung on its fixed support piece. Widely used with fin keels.

Spade rudder: Simply hung on its own shaft (stock) without further support. Used with fin keels.

Spi: Spinnaker.

Sports fisherman: Type of powerboat having large cockpit and flying bridge. Developed for big game fishing.

Sprayhood: Foldaway fabric shelter over companionway.

Stateroom: Marine version of 'master bedroom'.

Strip planked: Hull constructed of narrow planks fastened edge to edge producing carvel-like hull but without need for caulking.

Survey: Surveyor's report available for inspection.

TSDY: Twin screw (usually meaning also twin engines) diesel yacht.

t/flaps: Transom flaps. Outlets for water through stern of planing dinghy.

Teak: Highly durable hardwood. Trades Description Act has improved matters, but still have surveyor confirm that boat constructed of teak really *is*, since much wood that is 'like' teak is on the market.

Tender: Dinghy used for carrying crew and gear to and from yacht.

Trawler yacht: Type of motor cruiser with displacement hull and flying bridge.

Triple keel: Central ballast keel with twin bilge plates or unballasted aerofoil keels on either side.

vgc: Very good condition (according to owner).

VHF: Very high frequency radio for short range communications, either ship to ship or ship to shore.

VMG: Velocity (speed) made good, usually referring to electronic instrument that calculates same.

Vane steering: Wind operated self steering gear.

WEST: Wood Epoxy Saturation Technique. A trade name for a boatbuilding method whereby the hull is built using several layers of very thin veneers saturated in special epoxy resins. Produces very light, durable hulls.

W/house: Wheelhouse. A solid, permanent shelter over steering position.

Walker: Make of mechanical log.

Well found: Expression little used today meaning well equipped and implying fitness for seagoing.

Z-drive: Make of outdrive unit.

30×24×9×4 (for example): Dimensions of boat: LOA×LWL ×beam×draught. If only three dimensions given, these will be LOA, beam, draught.

+100 A1: A current classification at Lloyd's of London, covering all aspects of hull, machinery and gear.

3/4, 7/8, fractional: Description of rig where forestay terminates some distance below masthead.

Appendix B: Useful Addresses and Organisations

Association of British Yacht Agents (ABYA)
3 Twigsend Close
Sarisbury Green
Southampton SO3 6ET

Royal Yachting Association (RYA)
Victoria Way
Woking
Surrey GU21 1EQ

Ship and Boat Builders National Federation (SBBNF)
Boating Industry House
Vale Road
Oatlands Park
Weybridge
Surrey

Yacht Brokers, Designers and Surveyors Association (YBDSA)
Wheel House
Liphook
Hants GU30 7DW

Yacht Delivery Association
Tudor Cottage
Frampton
Dorchester
Dorset DT2 9NB

Appendix C: Sample Forms

Patrick Boyd Multihulls

Inholms Farm,
Horley,
Surrey, RH6 9DU

0293 773775

Yacht Name:

Type:	Flag:	**Machinery**
Date Built:	Registered:	Twin/Single Screw:
Built by:	At:	Make.
Designer:	Rig:	Diesel/Petrol:
Length O.A.:	Length W.L.:	Total h.p.
Beam:	Draught:	Fuel Capacity:
Material of Hull:		Consumption:
Deck:	Sheathed:	Generator:
Dinghy:		Electricity:

Machinery	
Twin/Single Screw:	Date:
Make.	No. of Cyl.:
Diesel/Petrol:	Reducing Gear:
Total h.p. at	R.P.M.
Fuel Capacity:	Max. Speed:
Consumption: Gal. per hr.:	
Lt. per hr.:	at Knots
Generator:	Date:
Electricity:	

Dinghy Engine:

Liferaft:

Spars:

Sails

Sails	Area sq. ft.	Maker	Year

Navigation

Echo Sounder:

R.D.F.:

Wind Speed & Dir.:

Close hauled Indicator:

Boat Speed & Log:

Radar:

R/T:

Automatic Pilot:

Distress Radio:

Other items of Equipment:

Where lying:

Price:

PLEASE TURN OVER FOR ACCOMMODATION DETAILS

147

Accommodation:

Cabin Berths:

Saloon Berths:

Quarter Berths:

F'c'sle Berths:

Total No. of Berths:

Showers: W.C.'s:

Galley:

Cooker:

Cold Storage:

Water Heater:

Water pressure feed:

Water quantity:

Accommodation Drawing:

Prescribed by the Commissioners of Customs & Excise with the consent of the Secretary of State for Trade

Form No. 10

X S 79

BILL OF SALE (Individuals or Joint Owners)

Official number	Name of Ship	Number, year and port of registry			Whether a sailing, steam or motor ship	Horse power of engines (if any)

Length from fore part of stem, to the aft side of the head of the stern post/fore side of the rudder stock

	Feet	Tenths

Main breadth to outside of plating

Depth in hold from tonnage deck to ceiling amidships

and as described in more detail in the Register Book.

	Number of Tons
	(Where dual tonnages are assigned the higher of these should be stated)
	Gross	Register

I/We (a) _____ the undersigned (b) _____ (hereinafter called "the transferor(s)")

in consideration of the sum of _____ paid to (c) _____ by (d) _____ (hereinafter called "the transferee(s)")

the receipt whereof is hereby acknowledged , transfer _____ shares in the Ship above particularly described, and in her boats and appurtenances, to the said transferee(s).

Further (e) _____ the said transferor(s) for (e) _____ heirs covenant with the said transferee(s) and

(f) _____ assigns, that (e) _____ have power to transfer in manner aforesaid the premises hereinbefore expressed to

be transferred, and that the same are free from encumbrances (g) _____

In witness whereof (e) _____ have hereunto subscribed (e) _____ name(s) and affixed (e) _____ seal on _____ 19 _____

Executed by the above named transferor(s)

in the presence of (f)

_____

_____ (Witness)

(j) _____   (Seal)

(a) "I" or "we". (b) Full name(s), address(es) and description of transferor(s). (c) "me" or "us". (d) Full name(s) and address(es) of transferee(s) with their description in the case of individuals, and adding "as joint owners" where such is the case, (e) "myself and my" or "ourselves and our". (f) "his", "their" or "its". (g) If any subsisting encumbrance add "save as appears by the registry of the said ship". (h) "my" or "our". (i) Name(s), address(es) and description of witness or witnesses. (j) Signature of transferor(s).

NOTE — A purchase of a registered British Vessel does not obtain a complete title until the Bill of Sale has been recorded at the Port of Registry of the ship; and neglect of this precaution may entail serious consequences.

NOTE — Registered Owners or Mortgagees are reminded of the importance of keeping the Registrar of British Ships informed of any change of residence on their part.

F 2059 (May 1979)

89377 Dd 586400 15M 5/79 StS.

149

YACHT SALE AGREEMENT

DATE   19

PARTIES

This Agreement is made between:

1.   of

         ("Seller")

     and

2.   of

         ("Buyer")

BROKER

The sale has been negotiated by   ("Broker")

which is a party to the Agreement for the purposes only of Clause 13.

SALE PARTICULARS

YACHT: Name:
        Description:
        Overall Length:
        Port of Registry and Official Order No:
        Port where now lying:

CLASSIFICATION
        Name of Authority:
        Class:
        Date of Expiry:

SEA TRIAL will*/will not* be required
        Arrangements as to:
        Date by which trial to be completed:

CONDITION SURVEY will*/will not* be required
        Arrangements as to:
        Date by which report to be completed: 19   */ days after the date for completion of the Sea Trial*

INVENTORY of outfit, gear, machinery and equipment to be as per the Inventory annexed to this Agreement or subsequently agreed between the Seller, or the Broker on his behalf, and the Buyer.

COMPLETION DATE: 19   */as specified in Clause 8A overleaf*

PLACE FOR COMPLETION:

PURCHASE PRICE:

DEPOSIT:

BALANCE OF PURCHASE PRICE:

*Delete as necessary

SPECIAL CONDITIONS:

1. The Seller shall sell and the Buyer shall purchase free from all charges and encumbrances the Yacht specified in the Sale Particulars together with all her outfit, gear, machinery and equipment on board or ashore, as specified in the Inventory (if any) but not including ship's stores or the Seller's personal effects, upon and subject to the terms and conditions of this Agreement including, where applicable, the Special Conditions specified.

2. Upon signature of this Agreement the Buyer shall pay to the Broker the Deposit in the currency specified in the Sale Particulars. The Broker shall hold the Deposit as stakeholder pending completion or cancellation of this Agreement, as the case may be.

3. As soon as practicable after signature of this Agreement, the Buyer shall check and settle the Inventory (if any) with the Seller or the Broker on the Seller's behalf.

4. On or before the date specified in the Sale Particulars for the completion of the Sea Trial (if any), the Seller and the Buyer shall take all necessary steps to conduct a Sea Trial at the Buyer's expense, in accordance with the arrangements specified in the Sale Particulars. On or before the day following the date so specified, the Buyer may, if dissatisfied with such Sea Trial, give to the Seller or the Broker notice of cancellation of this Agreement and the Seller shall thereupon without delay authorise the Broker to repay the Deposit, without interest, to the Buyer. If the Buyer fails to give such notice within the period specified he shall be deemed to be satisfied with the Sea Trial at the expiration of that period. Provided that if for any reason outside the control of the parties the Sea Trial cannot be completed by the date so specified the parties shall agree a reasonable alternative date therefor.

5. As soon as practicable after signature of this Agreement, the Buyer, if a Condition Survey is required, shall instruct a surveyor to carry out, at the Buyer's expense, a Condition Survey of the Yacht, outfit, gear, machinery and equipment in accordance with the arrangements, and submit his report by the date, specified in the Sale Particulars and the Seller shall make the Yacht available, afloat, for the Condition Survey in accordance with such arrangements. The Buyer may, at his expense, place the Yacht ashore or on a slipway or in dock and open up the Yacht for the purpose of the Condition Survey and shall, at his expense, close up, make good any damage caused and re-float the Yacht upon completion of the Condition Survey.

6. On or before the seventh (7th) day following the date specified in the Sale Particulars for completion of the Condition Survey report (if any), the Buyer may, if upon the Condition Survey material defects in the Yacht or her machinery have been found, give to the Seller or the Broker notice specifying or referring to such defects. If the Buyer fails to give such notice within the period specified he shall be deemed to be satisfied with the Condition Survey at the expiration of that period. Where the Buyer, being entitled so to do, gives such notice, the Buyer shall at the same time give to the Seller or the Broker either (i) notice of cancellation of this Agreement or (ii) notice of his willingness to proceed with the purchase subject either to such defects being made good at the Seller's expense or to a specified reduction in the Purchase Price. If the Buyer gives notice of cancellation, the Seller shall without delay authorise the Broker to repay the Deposit, without interest, to the Buyer. If the Buyer gives notice of his willingness to proceed with the purchase, subject as mentioned above, the Seller and the Buyer shall as soon as practicable agree for the defects to be made good by the Seller and, if the Buyer so requires, for the work to be certified by the surveyor or for the Purchase Price to be reduced but, if they are unable to agree, either of them may give to the other notice of cancellation of this Agreement and, upon giving or receiving such notice, the Seller shall without delay, authorise the Broker to repay the Deposit, without interest, to the Buyer.

7. Every representation, condition, warranty or other undertaking whether express or implied by statute, common law, custom or otherwise howsoever in relation to the Yacht, faults or errors in her description or her quality or her fitness for any particular purpose whether made or given before or after the date hereof is hereby excluded for all purposes.

8. Completion shall take place at the Place for Completion:
A. where a Condition Survey is required, by not later than the fifteenth (15th) day following the earliest of the following dates:—
   (i)   the date of receipt by the Seller of a notice from the Buyer that he is satisfied with the Condition Survey;
   (ii)   the date when, under Clause 6 above, the Buyer is deemed to be satisfied with the Condition Survey;
   (iii) the date of receipt by the Buyer of the Seller's notice (accompanied by the surveyor's certificate (if any)) that all material defects in the Yacht specified in the Buyer's notice under Clause 6 have been made good;
   (iv) the date upon which any reduction in the Purchase Price has been agreed between the Seller and the Buyer under Clause 6 above; or
B. where no Condition Survey is required, on the Completion Date specified in the Sale Particulars.

9. On completion:
   (i)   the Buyer shall pay the balance of the Purchase Price (less any agreed reduction) to the Broker as agent for the Seller by means of an approved banker's draft or transfer in favour of the Broker; and
   (ii)   the Seller shall deliver to the Buyer (a) the Yacht together with her outfit, gear, machinery and equipment, (b) a current classification certificate (where the Yacht is sold as being classified) and (c) a bill of sale and all such other documents as may be legally necessary effectively to transfer to the Buyer the ownership, free from all charges and incumbrances, of the Yacht.

10. The Yacht together with her outfit, gear, machinery and equipment shall remain at the risk of the Seller throughout the period until completion (including any period during which the Yacht is being made ready for or is undertaking any Condition Survey and/or Sea Trial pursuant to Clauses 4&5 above). If the Yacht be lost or irreparably damaged prior to completion this Agreement shall become null and void and the Deposit shall be refunded to the Buyer.

11. On completion, the Seller, if required by the Buyer, shall be responsible for effecting release of the present registration of the Yacht and supplying official evidence thereof and the Buyer shall be responsible for obtaining any new flag.

12. Failure by the Buyer to pay the balance of the Purchase Price upon the Completion Date shall entitle the Seller to charge interest thereon at the rate of ten per cent (10%) per annum from the due date until the date of actual completion or, by not less than seven (7) days' notice to the Buyer, to forfeit the Deposit and to treat this Agreement as having been repudiated by the Buyer and to recover from the Buyer all or any loss arising out of such repudiation. Failure by the Seller to comply with his obligations upon the Completion date shall entitle the Buyer, by not less than seven (7) days' notice to the Seller to treat this Agreement as having been repudiated by the Seller and to recover from the Seller all or any loss arising out of such repudiation.

13. The Seller and the Buyer each agrees with the Broker (a) that this sale has been negotiated and this Agreement has been entered into upon the Broker's Terms of Business current at the date hereof which shall apply (as if expressly set out herein) to all matters directly or indirectly arising out of or in connection with this Agreement and (b) that the Broker is a party to this Agreement for the purposes only of this Clause.

14. Any notice required or authorised to be given by either of the parties to the other may be given in any form of writing (including telegrams, cables or telex) and shall be deemed to be properly given if proved to have been despatched prepaid and properly addressed, in the case of a notice to the Seller, to him or the Broker at their respective addresses specified overleaf or in the case of a notice to the Buyer, to his address specified overleaf.

15. The validity, construction and performance of this Agreement shall be governed by the laws of England and the Seller and the Buyer each hereby submits to the non-exclusive jurisdiction of the High Court of Justice in England.

AS WITNESS the hands of the parties.

Witness   Seller . . . .

Witness   Buyer . . . .

Witness   Broker . . . .

Yacht Sale Agreement (contd)

PRESCRIBED BY THE COMMISSIONERS OF CUSTOMS AND EXCISE WITH THE CONSENT OF THE SECRETARY OF STATE FOR TRADE	Form No. 8	DECLARATION OF OWNERSHIP ON BEHALF OF A BODY CORPORATE	XS 72

Official number	Name of ship		Number, year, and port of registry

Whether a sailing, steam or motor ship		Horse power of engines, if any	

	Feet	Tenths
Length from fore part of stem, to the aft side of the head of the stern post/fore side of the rudder stock		
Main breadth to outside of plating		
Depth in hold from tonnage deck to ceiling amidships		

NUMBER OF TONS

* Gross	* Register	*Where dual tonnages are assigned the higher of these should be stated

and as described in more detail in the Certificate of the Surveyor.

I, the undersigned ....

of .... in the county of ....

(a) .... of .... Company, Limited,

declare as follows: – The said Company was incorporated by virtue of (b) ....

....

on the .... day of .... 19........................, and is subject to the laws of

(c) ....

The said Company has its principal place of business at ....

where all the important business of the Company is, in fact, controlled and managed at meetings of Directors or Managers of the Company.

The above described Ship was built at .... in the year ....

The general description of the Ship is correct ....

whose certificate of competency or service is No. ...., is Master of the said Ship.   The said Company is entitled

to be registered as owner of .... shares in the said Ship. To the best of my knowledge and belief, no person or body of persons other than such persons or bodies of persons as are by the Merchant Shipping Act, 1894, as amended by the British Nationality Act, 1948, qualified to be Owners of British Ships is entitled, as Owner, to any interest whatever, either legal or beneficial, in the said Ship. And I make this solemn Declaration conscientiously believing the same to be true.

Made and Subscribed the .... day

of .... 19 .... by the above-named

(d) ....

in the presence of (f) ....

(g) ....

....

at (h) ....

(e) ....

(a) Insert office of person making declaration, Secretary or otherwise.

(b) Here insert such of the descriptions as are applicable: –
"An Act of Parliament of the United Kingdom (cite the year of the reign in which the Act was passed, its chapter and title)",
or
"a Charter granted by H. Majesty and dated the .... day of .... 19 ...." or
"an Act or Ordinance of the Legislature of .... (cite the year in which the Act or Ordinance was passed, its chapter and title),"
or
"the Companies Act, 1948. (If incorporated before the commencement of the Act of 1948, the Act mentioned in the certificate of incorporation should be stated.)"

(c) The United Kingdom (or as the case may be). In the case of a Company incorporated by virtue of the Companies Acts, insert also "and its registered office is at ....
...."

(d) Give full name of declarant.

(e) Signature of declarant.

(f) Signature of person taking the declaration who should be a Registrar of British Ships, a Justice of the Peace, a Commissioner of Oaths within the meaning of the Commissioner for Oaths Acts 1889 and 1891 or a British Consular Officer.

(g) Full name and qualification of person taking the declaration.

(h) Place of attestation.

XS 72   F 1953 (Aug 1977)   MCR 14376/1/585726 4m 8/78 TL

Appendix C: Sample Forms

| PRESCRIBED BY THE COMMISSIONERS OF CUSTOMS AND EXCISE WITH THE CONSENT OF THE SECRETARY OF STATE FOR TRADE | Form No. 2 | DECLARATION BY INDIVIDUAL OWNER OR TRANSFEREE | X S 66 |

| Official number | Name of ship | | Number, year, and port of registry |

Whether a sailing, steam or motor ship | Horse power of engines, if any

| | Feet | Tenths |

Length from fore part of stem, to the aft side of the head of the stern post/fore side of the rudder stock ....

Main breadth to outside of plating ....

Depth in hold from tonnage deck to ceiling amidships   ....

NUMBER OF TONS

| *Gross | *Register | *Where dual tonnages are assigned the higher of these should be stated |

and as described in more detail in the Certificate of the Surveyor.

I, the undersigned (a).............................

.... declare as follows:—   I am a British Subject.

The above described Ship was built at ....   in the year ....

The general description of the Ship is correct ....

(name of Master)

whose certificate of competency or service is No. .... , is Master of the said Ship.   I am entitled

to be registered as owner of .... shares in the said Ship. To the best of my knowledge and belief, no person or body of persons other than such persons or bodies of persons as are by the Merchant Shipping Act, 1894, as amended by the British Nationality Act, 1948, qualified to be Owners of British Ships is entitled, as Owner, to any interest whatever, either legal or beneficial, in the said Ship. And I make this solemn Declaration conscientiously believing the same to be true.

Made and Subscribed the............................ day

of .... 19............ , by the above-named

(b)............................

in the presence of (d)............................   (c)............................

(e)............................

at (f)............................

(a) Here insert name, address and description of declarant.

(b) Give full name of declarant.

(c) Signature of declarant.

(d) Signature of person taking the declaration who should be a Registrar of British Ships, a Justice of the Peace, a Commissioner for Oaths within the meaning of the Commissioner for Oaths Acts 1889 and 1891, or a British Consular Officer.

(e) Full name and qualification of person taking the declaration.

(f) Place of attestation.

X S 66   F 1957 (Feb. 1977)   E.P 566509 10M 12/76

| PRESCRIBED BY THE COMMISSIONERS OF CUSTOMS AND EXCISE WITH THE CONSENT OF THE SECRETARY OF STATE FOR TRADE AND INDUSTRY | *Form No. 5* | DECLARATION BY JOINT OWNERS OR TRANSFEREES ATTENDING TOGETHER | X.S. 69 |

Official number	Name of ship	Number, year, and port of registry
		.

Whether a sailing, steam or motor ship	Horse power of engines, if any

	Feet	Tenths
Length from fore part of stem, to the aft side of the head of the stern post/fore side of the rudder stock		
Main breadth to outside of plating		
Depth in hold from tonnage deck to ceiling amidships		

NUMBER OF TONS

*Gross	*Register	* Where dual tonnages are assigned the higher of these should be stated

and as described in more detail in the Certificate of the Surveyor.

JOINT OWNERS

Name in full	Address	Occupation

Firstly — Each of us the several persons above-mentioned and whose names are hereunto subscribed declare as follows : I am a British Subject and my name and description as above given are true. The above described ship was built at

.... in the year .... The general description of the ship is

correct. .... whose certificate of competency or
(name of Master)

Service No. is .... is Master of the said ship.

Secondly — We the said several persons above-mentioned, respectively declare as follows:— We are entitled to be registered as

Joint Owners of .... shares in the said ship. To the best of our knowledge and belief, no person or body of persons other than such persons or bodies of persons as are by the Merchant Shipping Act, 1894, as amended by the British Nationality Act, 1948, qualified to be owners of British Ships is entitled, as Owner, to any interest whatever, either legal or beneficial, in the said Ship, and we, so far as relates to ourselves and each of us, make this solemn Declaration conscientiously believing the same to be true.

Made and Subscribed the .... day

of .... 19......., by the above-named

(a)
....

....   (b)
....

in the presence of (c)...

(d)
....

....

(a) Here insert full names of declarants i.e. the Joint Owners.

(b) Signatures of declarants.

(c) Signature of person taking the declarations who should be a Registrar of British Ships, a Justice of the Peace, a Commissioner for Oaths within the meaning of the Commissioner for Oaths Acts 1889 and 1891, or a British Consular Officer.

(d) Qualification of person taking the declaration and place of attestation.

Sec. F. 1956 (Dec. 1972)   Dmd. 176172 The C.C. Ltd. 4/74